The Gnosis of the Light

THE IBIS
WESTERN
MYSTERY TRADITION
SERIES

The heritage of all Western spirituality, both open and esoteric, and all the systems, theories, and practices that relate to it, are drawn from a single source: the Judeao-Christian spiritual tradition. This tradition has yet deeper roots in the distinctive religious faiths of the great civilzations of Egypt, Greece, and Mesopotamia.

At the heart of all these great traditions lies their ultimate goal: the spiritual regeneration of humanity. There is more than one Way to its attainment, and it is the totality of the many paths that lead us back to our primal source that constitutes the Western Mystery Tradition. They are encapsulated in the countless texts that enshrine and reflect the work of the inspired men and women who have dedicated their lives to preserving, interpreting, and transmitting this tradition.

Many of these text have become a part of the canon of Western literature, but there are many others that have been unjustly neglected, hidden in times of persecution, or have simply gone unrecognized. Some record exalted inner experiences, some are guides to esoteric practice, while others are speculative studies of esoteric knowledge and spiritual wisdom. All of them have one feature in common: an inherent power to enrich us spiritually.

It is from rare printed versions of these unknown or forgotten texts, and from studies of them, that the Ibis series of classics of the Western Mystery Tradition is drawn.

—The Editors of Ibis Press

The Gnosis of the Light

A Translation of the Untitled Apocalypse
Contained in the Codex Brucianus

With Introduction and Notes
by Rev. F. Lamplugh, B. A. (Cantab.)

Preface by R. A. Gilbert

Ibis Press
An Imprint of Nicolas-Hays, Inc.
Berwick, Maine

Published in 2006 by
Ibis Press, an imprint of
Nicolas-Hays, Inc.
P. O. Box 1126
Berwick, ME 03901-1126
www.nicolashays.com

Distributed to the trade by
Red Wheel/Weiser, LLC
65 Parker St Ste 7
Newburyport, MA 01950
www.redwheelweiser.com

Library of Congress Cataloging-in-Publication Data
available on request

Cover design by Kathryn Sky-Peck.
Typset in Dutch 766 BT
Printed in the United States of America.

12	11	10	09	08	07	06
7	6	5	4	3	2	1

VG

The paper used in this publication meets the minimum requirements of the American National Standard for Information Sciences—Permanence of Paper for Printed Library Materials Z39.48–1992 (R1997).

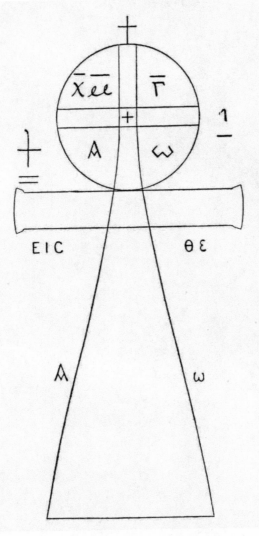

THE GNÔSTIC CROSS
(Codex Brucianus)

PREFACE

Gnosticism is an overworked term. Over the course of the last century it has been so misapplied, trivialised, and abused that it has become almost devoid of meaning, while a succinct and satisfactory definition of the word is now elusive almost to the point of being unattainable. And yet, unless we can establish a working meaning of Gnosticism—so that we have some idea of what Gnosticism is, and what the words "gnosis" and "Gnostic" mean—we shall fail utterly in any attempt at understanding "Gnostic" texts. So, what do these terms mean?

In loose, contemporary usage, the adjective "Gnostic" tends to be applied to any belief or pattern of thought that runs counter to the prevailing religious, philosophical, political, or social orthodoxy, and which justifies itself by appealing to a moral imperative grounded in "gnosis": a personal intuition or illumination derived directly from a spiritual, or non-specific and non-empirical authoritative source. Such applications are usually accompanied by an abdication of reason—and often of common sense as well—on the part of those who so apply them, and who frequently perceive themselves as being Gnostics, but tend to have the good grace not to appropriate the term "Gnosticism" to their particular beliefs.

To establish a satisfactory definition of that term, the first step must be to set the historical and cultural boundaries within which it will apply. Traditional perceptions of Gnosticism have seen it as being concerned with the beliefs and practices of certain groups of religious believers around the Mediterranean during the approximate period of the Roman Empire. There is no consensus among scholars as to whether these beliefs and practices originated within the Judaeo-Christian stream of faith, or outside it. And because of their great variety and complexity, there is debate as to the wisdom of using a single term, Gnosticism, to describe them.

What is certain is that the word itself is not ancient. It was coined in 1669 by the English theologian and Cambridge Platonist, Henry More (1614–1687), who used it in a pejorative way in the course of his polemic against Roman Catholicism, which was for him "a spice of the old abhorred Gnosticism." In More's sense, the word applied to the various heresies within the Christian Church described and—to their own satisfaction—refuted by Irenaeus, Hippolytus, and other early Church Fathers. But neither the heretics nor their opponents described their belief systems as "Gnosticism"; rather, it was γνωσις, a special kind of saving knowledge. Whether a particular brand of gnosis was perceived as true or false depended on one's religious perspective.

Thus, for Christians, gnosis was the knowledge of Christ's teaching and an acceptance of both His precepts and His offer to mankind of salvation by divine grace. In his Epistle to Timothy, St. Paul sets this against the "profane empty babblings, and opposing theories of the falsely named knowledge (γνώσεως), which some asserting have missed the mark concerning the faith" (1 Timothy 6:20). Of course, for believers in these many alternative "theories," their gnosis was anything but false. With such a broad base to the concept of gnosis, it is clearly unwise to treat these belief systems as a unitary whole. Other than Christianity, from which many of these systems unquestionably sprang, there was no underlying, all-embracing source religion, and thus no specific movement that merits the label "Gnosticism." It is, however, convenient for students and scholars of the many forms of gnosis prevalent in the early Christian centuries to use the word "Gnosticism" in a descriptive rather than a defining sense, as an umbrella under which may be gathered a constellation of belief systems, or schools of thought, that represent a particular type of religious tendency. Thus, at last, we begin to approach a meaning for "Gnosticism."

It must be stressed, however, that this loosely related cluster of Gnostic schools and systems had no single doctrine, or article of faith, common to all of them. Although their philosophical speculations and their practical expressions of religious feeling were—at least at first sight—sufficiently similar, or at least roughly analogous to one another, as to seem to be variations on a number of common themes, close examination reveals that there were just as many differences and contradictions as similarities. But, for better or worse, Gnosticism remains the descriptive label applied to these vanished faiths, and so we must set out the features of the most significant and distinctive of these common themes.

As with the followers of all religions, the Gnostics were concerned with the nature and inter-relationships of God, humans, and the universe, but in their way of perceiving, interpreting, and coming to terms with these, they differed radically from the major faiths of their day. Most of the Gnostics were dualists, believing that there was a distinction between the supreme, unknowable God—pure spirit, and the ultimate source of all—and the lesser, imperfect deity, the Demiurge (δημιουργός, lit., "Craftsman"), who had created matter: the world and everything in it, including the human race. Consequently humankind is imperfect and intrinsically evil, but there is an avenue of escape, a way of return to the true, unknowable God for the elite few within whom a spark of divine, spiritual substance is imprisoned. This spark can be liberated only through gnosis: the revealed secret knowledge that enables the knower to recognise his or her true self and to seek the ultimate goal of reintegration with the true God.

To attain that goal, three things are required: recognition of the divine spark within; reception of the revealed but secret knowledge that is gnosis; and the performance of the appropriate spiritual practices, which are reserved to illuminated Gnostics alone. Escape from matter is impossible for the unenlightened mass of humanity—they must remain prisoners of the Demiurge.

Such an élitist view of salvation runs counter to orthodox Christianity, for it rejects both salvation by faith alone, or in combination with works, and any form of Universalism. Inevitably, Gnostic views on the scriptures and on the person of Christ were also far from orthodox. The creator God of the Old Testament, the God of Israel, was perceived as being the Demiurge and was rejected utterly. Thus Christ, in his role as Savior and bearer of gnosis, could not be the son of such a God and could not assume a human body; nor could He have died upon the cross. Given these beliefs, it is not surprising that the early Church fathers condemned Gnostics as heretics.

From the historian's point of view this was fortunate, for the many anti-Gnostic writings of Irenaeus, Tertullian, Hippolytus, Epiphanies, and others provide us with detailed expositions of the doctrines, personalities, and activities of Gnostics from the 2nd to the 4th centuries. But they are also problematic texts, as polemic is never unbiased and even though extensive extracts from original Gnostic works are quoted, the reader can never be sure that what is written gives a complete and accurate portrayal of the true Gnostic ethos. They were, however, our only comprehensive source of information on the Gnostics for some fifteen hundred years.

By the end of the 4th century, the various Gnostic schools and systems had effectively faded away, victims less of persecution than of their own inherent reserve—elitist groups are not by nature evangelical—but one significant dualist religion based upon Gnostic thought did survive. Manichaeism, the religion of the Persian prophet Mani, arose in the 3rd century and survived, in China and Central Asia, until the 13th. This was a religion of absolute dualism, believing in equal and opposite eternal forces of light and dark, good and evil. While it was significantly different from what may be termed "classical" Gnostic religion, Manichaeism was the term used by orthodox controversialists to attack heretical movements within Christianity—Paulicians, Bogomils, and Cathars—that flourished in the early Middle Ages, and which were more closely allied to gnostic doctrines.

What is significant is that such heretics were termed "Manichees": they were not thought of as Gnostics. For the Christian church, the established religion of Western civilisation, the Gnostics were a problem of its early history, a problem solved and in no need of resurrection. Not until the seventeenth century, when Henry More created the term and Pierre Bayle incorporated it in his *Dictionnaire Historique et Critique* (1695), did "Gnosticism" reappear in speculative thought. Even then the Gnostics and their doctrines could be studied and judged only from patristic sources.

This situation changed in the mid to late 18th century, when two Coptic manuscripts of texts written by and for Gnostics themselves were discovered. Both of these are Coptic translations of lost Greek originals that were probably composed in the 3rd century. The first of them, the *Pistis Sophia*, surfaced about 1750 when it was bought from a London bookseller by Dr. Anthony Askew (1722–1774), a prominent classical scholar and collector of manuscripts. After his death the Codex Askewianus was acquired by the British Museum Library, but its earlier history is unknown.

The second manuscript, which contains the present text—the untitled Apocalypse that Lamplugh named *The Gnosis of the Light*—is now known as the Codex Brucianus. It was obtained in Egypt, probably in 1773, by the Scottish explorer and savant James Bruce, (1730–1794). The manuscript was purchased by Bruce at Medinet Habou, near the ancient Egyptian city of Thebes, when he passed through the place on his return journey from his travels in search of the sources of the Blue Nile. In 1848 it was bought by the Bodleian Library at the auction sale of Bruce's manuscripts. Precise details of its discovery have not been recorded, but according to the sale catalogue, it "had been found in the ruins near that place [Medinet Habou] in the former residence of some Egyptian monks."

Bruce left no account of his find, but Robert Curzon (1810–1873), a later collector of early Christian manuscripts who was at Thebes in 1833, gives a picturesque description of his adventures on a similar quest in his book, *Visits to Monasteries in the Levant* (revised edition, 1865). While there, Curzon learned of what seems to have been the same monastery:

> Not far from the ruins of the palace and temple of Medinet Habou stand the crumbling walls of an old Coptic monastery, which I was told had been inhabited, almost within the memory of man, by a small community of Christian monks. (p. 119)

His informant was a Coptic Christian, a carpenter, who told him a surprising tale.

> The carpenter related to me the history of the ruined Coptic monastery; and I found that its library was still in existence. It was carefully concealed from the Mohammedans,

as a sacred treasure; and my friend the
carpenter was the guardian of the volumes
belonging to his fallen church. After some
persuasion he agreed, in consideration of
my being a Christian, to let me see them.
(pp. 120–121)

The place was well concealed—an ancient tomb
with a half-concealed doorway—but to avoid
detection they went at night,

> . . . entered into the doorway of the tomb,
> and, passing through a short passage, found
> ourselves in a great sepulchral hall.... At the
> farther end of this chamber was a stone altar
> standing upon one or two steps, in an apsis
> or semicircular recess. (p. 122)

Here, to Curzon's delight, he saw that,

> The Coptic manuscripts, of which I was in
> search, were lying upon the steps of the altar,
> except one, larger than the rest, which was
> placed on the altar itself. They were about
> eight or nine in number, all brown and
> musty-looking books, written on cotton
> paper, or charter bombycina, a material in
> use in very early times. (p. 123)

Curzon did not take the books away—they were liturgies and martyrologies and he saw no sign of any Gnostic manuscripts, but his account of the library does indicate just how the Codex Brucianus may have survived the ravages of time and persecution.

A further century would pass before a third Coptic Gnostic manuscript—the two Ethiopic texts of *The Book of Enoch* that Bruce also brought back with him were neither ancient nor Gnostic—was discovered in 1896 at Akhmim, one hundred miles north of Thebes. This codex, which contains three Gnostic texts, the *Gospel of Mary*, the *Apocryphon of John*, and the *Sophia of Jesus Christ*, was acquired by the State Museum of Berlin and is known as the *Papyrus Berolinensis*. Fifty years after this codex came to light, our understanding of Gnostics and their faith was revolutionised by the discovery in 1945 of a Coptic Gnostic library at Nag Hammadi, in Upper Egypt.

The impact of this extraordinary find was not immediate, but as realisation of the significance of the Nag Hammadi texts grew, so academic and popular interest rapidly increased. The thirteen codices comprising this library were eventually brought together in the Coptic Museum in Cairo, after lengthy and complex commercial and academic negotiation, and a complete critical edition of texts and translations is gradually nearing completion. A complete English translation of the basic Nag Hammadi texts has also been available since 1977, but it should not be assumed that the earlier Gnostic texts have in any way been superseded. Both *Pistis Sophia* and the books in the Codex Brucianus are absent from the texts in the *Nag Hammadi Library*, and they are still crucially important for a full understanding of the Gnostic phenomenon.

Neither manuscript was known outside academic circles—and far from widely known within them—for a century and more after their discovery. They were both transcribed in the 1770s by the Coptic scholar C. G. Woide (1725–1790), but nothing appeared in print until a Latin translation of *Pistis Sophia*, by M. G. Schwarze, was published in 1851. A partial English translation followed in 1887, in C. W. King's *The Gnostics and Their Remains* (second edition, 1887); a French translation, by E. Amélinau, appeared in 1895, and in 1896 G.R.S. Mead published a complete English version. A critical edition of the Coptic text of *Pistis Sophia*, by Carl Schmidt, finally appeared in 1905. Publication of the Codex Brucianus lagged far behind.

Schwarze had transcribed the text in 1848, but he died before he was able to translate it and it was not until 1892 that the Coptic text was published, together with a German translation, in Schmidt's magisterial edition of the Codex Brucianus. In the previous year, Amélinau had issued his own edition of the text, but this was far from satisfactory, as he was unable to compare the rapidly deteriorating original with the copy made by Schwarze. An edition of the untitled text in the Codex, based on the original manuscript but making full use of Schmidt's transcript and with an annotated English translation, was made by Charlotte A. Baynes in 1933. Schmidt's edition of the full text was re-issued in 1978, with an English translation by Violet MacDermot.

These recent editions are of great importance as the Codex is unlikely to survive in the long term: seven of the 78 loose papyrus leaves of which it originally consisted are now missing, and those that are left have suffered from a century of maltreatment. Here it should be noted that the Codex is not a unitary work, but is made up of two quite distinct manuscripts—in different hands and on different types of papyrus—plus some additional, fragmentary material. Both are defective, and neither manuscript has a title, except for a line reading, "The Book of the great Logos corresponding to Mysteries" at the end of the first part of the longer one. It is generally referred to, however, as "The First and Second Books of Jeu," on the basis of a reference in *Pistis Sophia* to the "two Books of Jeu," which Schmidt concluded were the first two treatises contained in the Codex Brucianus. The second manuscript is the untitled Apocalypse that Lamplugh chose to call *The Gnosis of the Light*.

Once the Codex had been acquired by the Bodleian Library, it should have been in safe hands. Alas, it was not. The sad tale of its fate, summarised by Charlotte Baynes, does not make happy reading:

> In 1886 the authorities of the Bodleian Library caused the loose leaves of the Codex to be bound up in book form. Unfortunately the work was not supervised by a student of the Coptic language. There is neither order nor sequence among the leaves, while many are upside down and have the recto and verso reversed. At the same time the leaves were reduced in size, the ragged portions being trimmed off and removed. And further, four leaves [of the untitled text], in existence when Woide made his copy, disappeared, having perhaps been thrown out by the binder owing to their dilapidated condition. (p. xiv)

Worse was to follow. The paste used in binding the Codex led to damage from mildew, and despite subsequent efforts to eradicate this, deterioration of the papyrus has continued. In 1978 MacDermot noted that the manuscript,

> . . . is now unfortunately in very poor condition. The papyrus of many leaves is

> defective and there are opaque dark spots
> due to previous mildew. . . . The writing is
> so faded as to be almost illegible, even when
> viewed with ultra-violet light. (p. xi)

Perhaps the Codex will eventually be restored to something like its original state, but at the present time it seems to be on the road to extinction.

And so to the "Untitled Apocalypse" itself, Lamplugh's *Gnosis of the Light*. It is a truly remarkable example of the speculative thought of Gnostic theologians about the structure, history, and meaning of the ultimate heaven, and about the nature of God. This is not apocalypse in the sense of prophetic history, but rather as a visionary journey through the heavenly worlds, recounted in complex and colorful imagery. For this reason, Michel Tardieu, a contemporary scholar of Gnosticism, has suggested that it be called the *Celestial Topgraphy*. But who was the author? To which Gnostic school or system did he belong, and why did he write this text?

There can be no definitive answers to these questions, but although it is far from orthodox, the *Gnosis of the Light* is unquestionably Christian in its ethos. It has been argued by some modern scholars that it is a Sethian text, produced within a body of Gnostics who believed that salvation is reserved to the descendants of Seth, Adam's third and righteous son. Whether or not there really was

such a distinct group is still a subject of debate, and
it has been pointed out, by Charlotte Baynes and
others, that the text has much in common with the
system of Valentinus, the second-century Egyptian
Gnostic whose systematic theology contains all
the classical features commonly found under the
umbrella of Gnosticism. Ultimately the question of
authorship does not matter for the lay reader, who
is concerned far more with the content of the text.
It was for such readers, visionary, grounded in the
spiritual world and with a preference for asceticism,
that the text was designed.

And it was unquestionably for such individuals
that Lamplugh produced his translation. It is
unfortunate that he should have used Amélinau's
French translation, published in 1891 with his
edition of the text, rather than Schmidt's far
superior version in German, but this does not
detract from either his introduction or his notes.
For Lamplugh, *The Gnosis of the Light* is a perfect
literary expression of those subjective forms of
spirituality that have descended from the first
centuries of this era, and which cannot convey
their enriching message save in highly symbolic
language. Such texts require an interpreter and
expositor, and it was these roles that Lamplugh
took upon himself. Other editors and translators
of the "Untitled Apocalypse" have approached the
text as historians and analysts of a dead system;
only Lamplugh has treated it as a living text of real

spiritual value. And it is primarily for this reason that his little book deserves to be more widely known and savored.

But who was this obscure Anglican priest who entered so wholeheartedly into Gnostic spirituality? From the language and references in his notes it is clear that Lamplugh was well-versed in the spirituality of the Western Hermetic Tradition, and was familiar with the terminology of esoteric Freemasonry. Of his life, almost nothing is known.

The Rev. Alfred Amos Fletcher Lamplugh was the vicar of St. John's at Newtown in the city of Leeds. In 1909, he had applied for admittance to A. E. Waite's Independent and Rectified Rite of the Golden Dawn (although there is no evidence that he actually entered the Order) and in 1915 he published a small book on *Some Aspects of Mysticism in Islam*.

Beyond this, and of greater significance, he had been heavily influenced by G.R.S. Mead, whose work he frequently utilises, and duly acknowledges, in his own text. Mead in turn gave Lamplugh due praise in his review of *The Gnosis of the Light* in *The Quest* (vol. 9, no. 4 [1918]: 674–675), recommended the book to his readers, and made his own comment on the merits of the text:

> In the midst of obscurities there appear
> passages of such great beauty as to make

immediate appeal to lovers of the mystical
element in religion.

At least one of his readers took Mead's words
to heart. Charlotte Baynes owed equally as much to
Mead as did Lamplugh. In the preface to her edition
of the Untitled Apocalypse, she acknowledges that
it was Mead, "who by his writings and lectures
inspired me with a desire to work on the subject of
Christian Gnosticism" (p. x). Thus it was Mead,
whose extracts from the *Untitled Apocalypse* in his
Fragments of a Faith Forgotten (1900) were the first
appearance in English of any of the text, who had
unwittingly inspired their full translation not once,
but twice. But it was only Lamplugh who poured his
heart as well as his mind into the work.

R. A. Gilbert,
Bristol, England
December 2005

INTRODUCTION

This translation of the ancient Gnôstic work, called by Schmidt, the *Untitled Apocalypse*, is based chiefly on Amélineau's French version of the superior MS. of the Codex Brucianus, now in the Bodleian Library, Oxford. In making the rendering I have studied the context carefully, and have not neglected the Greek words interspersed with the Coptic; also I have availed myself of Mr Mead's translation of certain important passages from Schmidt's edition, for purposes of comparison. Anything that I have added to bring out the meaning of the Gnôstic author now and again, I have enclosed in brackets. Such suggestions have always arisen from the text. I fancy my English version will be found to give a reasonably accurate idea of the contents of one of the most abstruse symbolical works in the world. The notes that I have added are not intended to be final or exhaustive, but to give the general reader some guidance towards understanding the intensely interesting topics with which the powerful mind of the ancient mystical writer was preoccupied. I have endeavoured to show myself a sympathetic "Hierophant" or expounder of some of the mysteries, not without study of the Gnôsis, both of the Christianised and purely Hellenistic type, for the key to the understanding of symbolism is only given into the hands of sympathy.

The Codex Brucianus was brought to England from Upper Egypt, by the famous traveller Bruce, in 1769, and bequeathed by him to the care of the Bodleian Library, Oxford. It contains several Gnôstic works translated into the Upper Egyptian dialect from the Greek, and probably is as old as the sixth century A.D. The Greek originals were of course much older, that is to say, the MSS. to which the codex ultimately goes back were much older. We are only concerned with one of them here, the so-called *Untitled Apocalypse*, which is markedly distinct from the others in character and style. Schmidt dates it well in the second century A.D., and with this estimate I am inclined to agree. It shows, as I have endeavoured to make clear in the notes, marked affinities in some respects to the *Gospel of Mary* (Codex Akhmim), which we know to have been in existence before 180 A.D., and its philosophical basis is the Platonism of Alexandria. If it is by one writer, I think it may be dated from 160 or 170 A.D.–200 A.D., and belongs to the period of Basilides and Valentinus.

Before venturing upon any discussion of the authorship and contents of our document, it would be as well to say a few words as to the meaning of that much misunderstood technical term "Gnôsis" in Hellenistic and early Christian theology. For a fuller exposition I would refer the reader to the admirable essay upon the subject by Mr G.R.S. Mead in his volume *Quests Old and New*. Gnôsis was not "philosophy" in the generally accepted sense of the term, or even religio-philosophy. "It was immediate knowledge of God's mysteries received from direct intercourse with the Deity—mysteries which must remain hidden from the natural man, a knowledge at the same time which exercises decided reaction on our relationship to God and also on our nature or disposition" (Reitzenstein). It was the power or gift of receiving and understanding revelation, which finally culminated in the direct unveiled vision of God and the transformation of the whole man into spiritual being by contact with Him. The ground of the idea of Gnôsis does not seem to be very different from that of the later "Mystical Theology," "which originally meant the direct, secret, and incommunicable knowledge of God received in contemplation" (Dom John Chapman). The revelation sought for was not so much a dogmatic revelation as a revelation of the processes of "transmutation" of Rebirth, of Apotheosis or "Deification." Its aim was dynamic rather than static. But while the followers of the Gnôsis, both Christian and Hellenistic, would have agreed that the direct knowledge of God is incommunicable to others, they undoubtedly seem to have held that there were what may be described as intermediate or preparatory processes or energisings which could be communicated: (1) by initiation into a holy community; (2) by a duly qualified master; (3) under the veils of symbols and sacraments.

The Gnôstic movement began long before the Christian era (what its original historical impulse was we do not know), and only one aspect of it, and that from a strictly limited point of view, has been treated by ecclesiastical historians. Recent investigations have challenged the traditional outlook and the traditional conclusions and the traditional " facts." With some to-day, and with many more to-morrow, the burning question is, or will be—not how did a peculiarly silly and licentious heresy rise within the Church—but how did the Church rise out of the great Gnôstic movement, and how did the dynamic ideas of the Gnôsis become crystallised into Dogmas? I do not indicate a solution; I do not express an opinion. I call attention to a fact in the world of scholarship that will not be without its decided reaction upon the plain man. But the study of the ancient Gnôsis, and indeed of mysticism generally, has left another suggestion that seems laden with limitless possibilities. Let us first go back to what I said as to the communication of certain "processes," "leavenings," or "energisings" under a sacramental veil. These processes were held to modify the nature of the person who submitted to them in a peculiar manner that was likened to the impress or "character" of a seal upon wax. These seals or "characters" could not only be acquired through formal rites and by the laying on of the hands of a master, but also, I am disposed to believe, by a certain mode of study—I am developing the Gnôstic theory, not stating one of my own—namely, that of a highly symbolic literature. The objection of the Gnôstic to a plain statement of facts would probably be somewhat as follows: "What you say is very good and true as far as it goes, but it is 'Pistis,' not Gnôsis; Faith, not Knowledge. You desire to be a changed man. Pistis will change you to a certain extent. I have nothing to say against it, but it will not change you in the radical way that Gnôsis does." If you went on to argue that your statement was reasonable and received admirable support from logic and philosophy, he would probably reply: "Philosophy of the kind you mention is excellent, and forms a basis for Gnôsis which is not contrary to reason, though it is above it. Gnôsis is a rebirth by which you become a god, and then you will have no need to find out things by talking and discursive reasoning, for everything will be within yourself and you will know all things in a vital way, by an act of simple intuition in the end. 'The wind bloweth where it listeth, and thou hearest the sound thereof, but canst not tell whence it cometh, and whither it goeth; so is every one that is born of the Spirit.' If you tie yourself down to logic, you will not know the real things, the 'Things that are,' by getting inside them. Your knowledge will be external, superficial. Gnôsis, you may be surprised to learn, is not just 'knowing,' it is light and 'life,' living and being as

well. This must not be taken as an attacking reason; if you join our school you will have a stiff course of Plato. You ought to know the 'Things that are' from the ordinary point of view, from outside, before you approach them with the idea of getting inside them, and so raising them up within yourself as far-shining lives. Afterwards you will study in a new manner that will seem madness to the common-sensed; and a Divine Madness indeed it is, for it will lead you to the secret of the Cross."

Hence the disciple was confronted in due time with a document that would not yield its secrets to dialectic, a kind of ritual in words that initiated his intuition into self-knowledge. Intense devotion was needed, imagination, and will-power. The Gnôsis came gradually, perhaps after the manuscript had been laid aside; it was the effort towards a sympathetic understanding that mattered, that was rewarded with life and light from God. The mere success of the logical mind in unravelling a puzzle was as nothing, for the readings of these monstrous, many-faceted stars of symbolism were infinite. That the intuition should enter into self awareness as into a sacred place of the mysteries—that was a process of the Gnôsis.

Now this strange way of teaching, which was really a "Cloud of Unknowing," was the real basis and point, as it were, of the Alexandrine method of interpreting Scripture. Think of Philo and what he says of the teaching of his Gnôstic

Therapeuts. Think of Clement, and of Origen with his "Eternal Gospel." This quickening of the intuition into knowledge of itself and God, through allegory and symbol based on philosophy, was the Everlasting Gospel.

So Gnôstic documents were not merely intended to puzzle the outsider, but the insider as well. This fact will enable us to appreciate better Basilides' famous remark about the one or two only who could understand his system. His frame of mind was a little like that of a university examiner after setting a paper. We need not think that these people were altogether destitute of humour. It would be a gross exaggeration, of course, to say that all the Gnôstic systems described in Irenacus and Hippolytus might have been devised by the same man, but it would be a useful exaggeration, illustrating the extreme anti-literalist point of view. Our knowledge of the schools rests for the most part on reports made upon documents such as these, the purport of which was entirely missed by those that made them. They treated Gnôsis as if it were another kind of "Pistis," or another system of philosophy. One doubts very much the correctness of the traditional classification of schools, which was made by people who were not in very close touch with them. One doubts if there was much hostility between these schools, however much their symbolism may appear to differ on the surface.

What was the result of these processes "initiated" or "started" by sacramental rites, by symbolism, by masters of Gnôsis? Was the result something purely "subjective" at best? The answer of the Masters of the Gnôsis to this question, which is characteristic of the modern mind and expresses the doubt which is gnawing at the heart of much modern religious life, would have been "No. There are certain physical changes as well. The body is spiritualised." They might possibly have added, "It is assumed, in part at least, by the Body of Stars[1] which has been awakened within it. This is the Body by means of which Union with God takes place, and then still more wonderful changes happen. We can awaken the Body of Stars or Rays, but to unite it with Himself, that depends upon the Will of God above, but all is a mystery of Grace."

This awakening of the Body of Stars, this assumption, or partial assumption, by immortality of the inner flesh, is the interesting possibility to which I referred earlier. Let me here quote two Catholic writers. Says Döllinger (*First Age*, p. 235, quoting Rom. vii. 22, I Cor. vi. 14, Eph. iii. 16 and 30, in support), "Saint Paul not only divides man into body and spirit, but distinguishes in the bodily nature, the gross, visible, bodily frame and a hidden, inner 'spiritual' body not subject to limits of space or cognisable by the senses; this last,

[1]   Not to be confused with the "astral body" of modern theosophy.

which shall hereafter be raised, is alone fit for and capable of organic union with the glorified body of Christ, of substantial incorporation with it." Dom John Chapman, O.S.B., in his excellent article on "Catholic Mysticism" in Hastings' *Encyclopædia of Religion and Ethics*, vol. ix., writes: "It is not to be denied that this psycho-physical side demands scientific investigation. It seems certain that St John of the Cross is justified in his view that the body is somehow 'spiritualised' by contemplation. Such facts as the power of saints over the animal world and the power of reading thoughts, *e.g.*, are proved beyond cavil."

Here, then, we have a consistent tradition held by many schools, and I think that it is by investigation along the lines suggested by Dom John Chapman that there is the greatest chance of arriving at some proof of immortality that will satisfy the scientific mind. For the claim of mystics is that here and now it is possible to participate consciously in that which is immortal, and the "spiritualising" of the body is an outward sign of the substantiality of that claim, the standard set up upon a hill to testify that the human consciousness is not planetary merely, not "hylic," nor "psychic," but has its root in the wisdom that issues from an inconceivable Abyss of Life and Light.

I believe that the original source of the document I have translated belonged to an Egyptian community or school of contemplation whose name has been forgotten in the night of time; that it was connected with the preparation of a candidate for the Baptism of Light. What form this rite really took it is impossible to say, but that it had outward signs of some kind is extremely probable. We have an old Gnôstic ritual preserved in the compilation generally known as the "Acts of John." Perhaps this may give us some idea of the sort of ceremony that was worked: I fancy there was an Eucharistic side, and that the Baptism of Light was connected with the mystic crucifixion alluded to so often in the notes. Possibly in the midst of the sacred dance, at the breaking of the Bread, there was a certain laying on of hands by an adept Master, one who had himself attained to the autoptic vision, and then the candidate was left alone to immerse himself in the Dark Ray of the Divine Mind.

I think also that the original MS. was based upon the work of one Master, whose name, like that of the order to which he belonged, is lost in the night of time, but that it also contains amplifications and additions by at least one later hand. It will thus represent the mind of a grade of teaching, and possibly contains material dating back to the period of the Therapeutæ that Philo knew. In other words, the community may have been an old one before it was Christianised. In any case, it remains the record of a stupendous spiritual adventure, the attempt to produce a race of Divinised men, that is not without the splendour of tragedy, for at some

time, like the Holy Cup of Legend, the presence of
Masterhood departed, and the external house fell
into ruin and its place knew it no more. Perhaps,
in the desire to propagate, it admitted unworthy
candidates; perhaps it turned to the by-ways of
magic in an attempt to arrest the external course of
nature and to defy necessity; perhaps there came a
day when none could understand the inner meaning
of the high and far-shining mysteries, and so amidst
party strife the building word was lost. Many a man,
no doubt, who called himself a "Gnôstic" was but
a sorry rogue; many another was but a student of
the letter, not of the life; many another was but a
spiritual swashbuckler, pompous in his demeanour
and cryptic in his utterance; some, led by an
abhorrent fantasy, may have wandered along the
path that goes to the Venus-berg and have striven
to lisp a formula that would transform the earth
into Gehenna rather than into Heaven. But, beside
this mass of imposture, of folly, of elegant idleness
and of corruption, the *à rebours* of a spiritual
outpouring, there was a real mysticism that could
present the Authentic Spectacle and could utter
comfortable words in tongues not of this world
utterly. There was a Gnôsis that strove to give the
Peace of God to those within and to those without,
because in Peace all things were made, that yearned
to bring forth children, quickened fiery souls, æons,
gods, in bodies of light for the love of God; that saw
in all things Grace, the Sponsa Dei, the Mother

most pure and immaculate. "No creature was ever
wronged of Thee," no spark ever quenched, no hope
defrauded and hurled eternally from the sky with
shattered wings by Thee. Such is the fair Faith that
chanted its prayer beneath a heaven set with such
strange galaxies, and whispers to us now through
the disremembered symbols of a forgotten book.

It is pleasant, in these days of strife, to be able
to quote Dr Schmidt's appreciation of the *Untitled
Apocalypse* with a cordial agreement:

"What a different world, on the contrary, meets
us in our thirty-one leaves! We find ourselves in the
pure spheres of the highest Plêrôma; we see, step by
step, this world, so rich in heavenly beings, coming
into existence before our eyes; each individual
space with all its inmates is minutely described,
so that we can form for ourselves a living picture
of the glory and splendour of this Gnôstic heaven.
The speculations are not so confused and fantastic
as those of the Pistis Sophia and our two Books of
Jeu.... The author is imbued with the Greek spirit,
equipped with a full knowledge of Greek philosophy,
full of the doctrine of the Platonic ideas, an adherent
of Plato's view of the origin of evil—that is to say,
Hyle.... We possess in these leaves a magnificently
conceived work by an old Gnôstic philosopher, and
we stand astonished, marvelling at the boldness
of the speculations, dazzled by the richness of the
thought, touched by the depth of soul of the author.
This is not, like the Pistis Sophia, the product of

declining Gnôsticism, but dates from a period when Gnôstic genius, like a mighty eagle, left the world behind it and soared in wide and ever wider circles towards pure light, towards pure knowledge, in which it lost itself in ecstasy.

"In one word, we possess in this Gnôstic work, as regards age and contents, a work of the very highest importance, which takes us into a period of Gnôsticism, and therefore of Christianity, of which very little knowledge has been handed down to us."

Finally, I wish to acknowledge my indebtedness to the scholarship of Mr G.R.S. Mead, whose labours in the field of Hellenistic Theology have to my mind received insufficient recognition, and whose admirable translations I have often used in the notes.

The Gnôsis
of the
Light

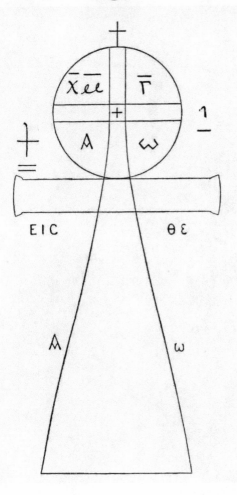

The Gnôsis of the Light

†THIS is the Father of all Fathers, the God of all . . . Gods, Lord of all Lords, Sonship of all Sons, Saviour of all Saviours, Invisible of all Invisibles, Infinity of all Infinities, Uncontainable of all Uncontainables, Beyond-the-Deep of all Beyond-the-Deeps, Space of all Spaces. This is the Spiritual Mind which existed before all Spiritual Minds, the Holy Place comprehending all Holy Places, the Good comprehending all Goods. This is the Seed of all good things. It is He who has brought them all forth, this Autophues or Being who has produced Himself, who existed before all the beings of the Plêrôma which He Himself has brought forth, Who is in all time. This is that Ingenerable and Eternal One who has no name and who has all names; who was the first to know those of the Universe, who has looked upon those of the Universe, who has heard those of the Universe. He is mightier than all might, upon whose incomprehensible Face no one is able to gaze. Beyond all mind does He exist in His own Form, Solitary and Unknowable. The Universal Mystery is He, the Universal Wisdom, of all things the Beginning. In Him are all Lights, all Life, and all Repose. He is the Beatitude of which all

---

† The title and the opening part of the work are lost.

in the Universe are in need, for that they might receive
Him they are. All beings of the Universe does He
behold within Himself, that One Uncontainable, who
parts those of the Universe and receives them all into
Himself. Without Him is nothing, for all the worlds
exist in Him, and He is the boundary of them all. All
of them has He enclosed, for in Him is all. No Space
is there without Him, nor any Intelligence; for without
that Only One there exists nothing. The Eternities
(æons) contemplate His incomprehensibility which
is within them all, but understand it not. They wonder
at it because He limits them all. They strive towards
the City in which is their Image. In this City[1] it is that
they move and live [and have their true being]; for it
is the House of the Father, the Robe of the Son, and
the Power of the Mother, the Image of the Plêrôma.
He is the First Father of all things, the First Eternal,

[1]   The centre of the Universe, which is everywhere and
nowhere; the ideal unity in diversity, from which all things
flow out and into which all things return. Just as Jerusalem
was held to be the centre of the earth, so was this "City" held
to be the hidden centre of the Universe; hence it is often
named "Jerusalem Above, who is the Mother of us all." It is
the principle at once of universality and individuality, the real
"ground" or centre of the soul. It is called the "House of the
Father" because it is the abiding place of the Presence; the
"Robe of the Son" because it is His Body of Manifestation
(cp. 2 Clem. xiv.); the "Power of the Mother" because it is the
"Energy" by which man is reborn into Divine consciousness;
and the "Image or Archetype of the Plêrôma" (the World of
Eternal Ideas in their "Fullness"), because it is the Wisdom
which is the basis of all consciousness.

the King of those that None can Touch; He in whom all things lose themselves, He who has given all things form within Himself; the Space which has grown from Itself, He who is born of Himself, the Abyss of all being, the Great and True One who is in the Deep; He in whom the Fullnesses (Plêrômata) did come, and even they are silent before Him. They have not named Him, because Unnamable and beyond thought is He, that First Fount whose Eternity stretches through all Spaces, that First Tone[2] whereby all things hearken and understand. He it is whose limbs make a myriad, myriad Powers, and every Power is a being in itself.

The Second Space is that which is called Creator, Father, Word, Source, Mind, Man, Eternal, Infinite. He is the Pillar, the Overseer, the Father of all. He it is upon whose Head the æons form a crown, darting forth their rays. The Fullness of His Countenance is

2   This term rather suggests the use of a vibratory formula to induce certain interior states as a practice of the School to which the Greek MS. belonged. Perhaps this may have been ÏAÔ, the meaning of which is given elsewhere as "Ï, because the All (or Plêrôma) hath gone forth. A, because it will turn itself back again. Ô, because the consummation of all consummations will take place." This may be taken to mean exoterically, "Ï, the Incarnation of Jesus, Who is the Plêrôma. A, the Crucifixion. Ô, the Ascension." Taken esoterically, it may mean, "Ï, the Soul, has come forth from God into generation. A, it is started or "Initiated" on its return journey through the Life of the Cross. Ô, there is union with God in the Eternity of Eternities as the consummation of all things" (cp. note 18). The work we are studying might almost be considered an exposition of this formula, though I do not

unknown to the external worlds who seek His Face,
for evermore yearning to know It, for unto them His
Word has run forth and to behold It is their desire.
The Light of His Eyes pierces to the spaces of the
external Plêrôma and the Word goes forth from His
Mouth to those who dwell in Heaven and to those
who dwell beneath it. The hairs of His Head are the
number of the Hidden Worlds, and the Features
of His Face are the type of the Eternities; the
hairs of His Beard are the number of the External
Worlds. The stretching out of His Hands is the
manifestation of the Cross.[3] The strain of the Cross
is the Ennead, the Ninefold Being. He who springs

suggest that it literally is so. We begin by reading it from right
to left, beginning with the God "beyond Name," that is He
whose being cannot be expressed by any name, Ô. We pass
to the Logos, the Divine Mind, He who can be named, and
His Plêrôma, A, from which is "started" the Visible World by
the going forth of the "Light-Spark" or "Man," Ï. After this
we read from left to right, but this is the expounding of the
mystical life, the "return," under a veil of symbolism. ÏAÔ is
the great Name of God in three vowels, derived historically,
no doubt, from the Great Name in Judaism, and is the
counterpart of the Indian AUM. Probably, like this latter,
it was pronounced in three ways: (1) audibly; (2) inaudibly
to others, but with the lips; (3) mentally. It was a formula
of a sacramental kind by which the life of the disciple was
mystically identified with the Life of the Master, so that the
knowledge of the real nature of the soul is given or restored
by God. During its use the mind was, of course, concentrated
on its inner meanings. Various aspects of mystical truth could
be expressed by its permutations: ÏAÔ, ÔAÏ, AÔÏ, etc.

[3]   *Cp*. Odes of Solomon, 27: "I stretched out my hands and

up [? or is nailed] to the right and to the left of the Cross is the Man whom no man can comprehend. He is the Father, the Fount whence Silence wells, He for whom the Quest is everywhere. The Father is He from whom went forth the Monad and the Spark of Light, and before this all the Worlds were dark nothings. For it is that Spark of Light which has placed all things in the rays of Its Splendour, so they have received Knowledge [Gnôsis], Life, Hope, Peace, Faith, Love and Resurrection, the Second Birth and the Seal. Now these things are the Ennead, the Ninefold Being, which has come forth from the Father without beginning, who alone has

worshipped the Lord, for the extension of my hands is His sign, and my expansion is the Upright Tree [or Pillar]."

The Cross of Calvary was taken, by the Gnôstics, to be the outward and visible sign of a concealed or Cosmic Cross, another aspect of the "City" or Monad, upon which the Logos or Light-Spark, as the "Son of Man," or the "Man," was crucified perpetually in an ineffable manner, thus communicating His Life and Light to the Universe. The substance or "strain" of this Cross is symbolised here by the Ennead or Ninefold Being, the members of which, Knowledge, Life, Hope, etc., are each in themselves Ideal Beings, Eternities, or Gods. Yet these Nine, a number typical of Initiation, are also one, as the Master and the Cross are also one. The Mystery is that of an Unbloody Sacrifice once and perpetually offered and also of Divine Espousal. [See further the " Hymn of Jesus " and the "Gnôstic Crucifixion" texts and commentaries by G. R. S. Mead, who renders the passage in the text by "The Source of the Cross is the Man whom no man can comprehend."]

been His own Father and His own Mother, whose
Plêrôma surrounds the twelve[4] Deeps.

The First Deep is the Universal Fount, from
whom all fountains have gone forth.

The Second Deep is the Universal Wisdom,
from whom all wisdoms have gone forth.

The Third Deep is the Universal Mystery, from
whom all mysteries have gone forth.

The Fourth Deep is the Universal Gnôsis, from
whom all Gnôses have gone forth.

The Fifth Deep is the Universal Purity, from
whom all purity has gone forth.

The Sixth Deep is the Silence that contains all
silences.

The Seventh Deep is the Universal Super-
essential Essence, from whom all essences have
gone forth.

The Eighth Deep is the Forefather from whom
and by whom all forefathers exist.

[4]   "Twelve" seems to symbolise the Powers creative of all
kinds of life in their totality, the creative imagination or raying
forth power.

The Ninth Deep is the All-Father, Self-Father, in whom is the All-Paternity of those who are Self-Fathers of the all.

The Tenth Deep is the All-Power, from whom all powers have gone forth.

The Eleventh Deep is that in which there is the First Invisible, from whom have gone forth all invisibles.

The Twelfth Deep is the Truth, from whence all truths have sped forth.

Now the Truth[5] which envelops all things is the Image of the Father, the End of all things. She is the Mother of all Eternities, who surrounds all Deeps, the Monad beyond knowledge who cannot be known, without seal-mark and having all seal-marks within, blessed for ever and ever. To the Father Ineffable, Inconceivable, Unthinkable, Unchangeable, all things have been made like in

[5]   "Truth" is another name for the Bride of the Logos, His "Great Surround" or Body. It is the Divine Concept or Conceiving Thought of the Cosmos and its processes, and hence it is also the seal of perfection or Body of Glory, the Life with which the Risen and Ascended Master is clad. While conferring character on all things, it is entirely transcendent, modeless, and "un-walled." Through it God is immanent in the Universe, hence it is also called "Mother." This is what the symbolism seems to imply.

their being. They rejoiced and have been filled with life-giving powers. They engendered myriads and myriads and myriads of æons, and in Joy, because they rejoiced with the Father.[6]

These are the worlds from which the Cross upsprang, and from their incorporeal limbs the Man has come forth. It is the Father and Fount of all being who has produced the limbs.

Now from the Father are all names,[7] whether Ineffable One, or Incorruptible One, or Invisible One, or Simple One, or Solitary One, or Powerful One, or Triple-powered One, or the names that in Silence alone are named. In the Father are they all, and He it is whom the Outer Worlds behold [as men behold] the starry sky at night. Even as men [so gazing into the night] desire to see the Sun, so do the Outer Worlds desire to see Him because of the very Invisibility which surrounds Him. He it is who to the æons gives life perpetually, and by His

[6]   This implies the doctrine of the Macrocosm and the Microcosm, of the Universe and of the individual soul as a perfect compendium thereof. All the great cosmic processes are to be found within the soul.

[7]   A "name" was held to be that which manifests the innermost essence of a thing. Hence it symbolised the spiritual body or ideal vehicle of manifestation, the life clothing. The bestowal of a new name is therefore the sacramental sign of the gift of a new body or mode of life. The real and ineffable Name of God is the Concept or Conceiving Thought referred to in note 5. But this is the Name "Mother" or "Bride" of the Logos, Providence. To "name" was a sacramental way of invoking a presence or "spiritual vehicle."

Word hath the Indivisible ... the Monad in order to
know it. For it is by His Word that the Holy Plêrôma
exists. This is the Father, the Second Creator, by the
breath of whose Mouth Providence (Pronoia) has
been in travail of those who were not, and it is by His
Will that they are. ... This is the Father, Ineffable,
Unspeakable, Beyond Knowledge, Invisible,
Immeasurable, Infinite. He has produced those that
are in Him within Himself. The Thought of His
Greatness has He brought forth from non-being
that He might make them to be. Incomprehensible
is He in His limbs. A Space has He made for His
limbs that they might dwell in Him and know Him
for their Sire. From His First Thought[8] has He
made them come forth, and she has become a Space
for them and given them being. ...

In this wise has He created the Temple of the
Plêrôma. At the four gates of the [Temple of] the
Plêrôma are four Monads, a Monad at each gate, and

---

[8]   *Cp*. Codex Akhmim: "Of Him it is said, He thinketh His
Image alone and beholdeth it in the Water of Pure Light which
surroundeth Him. And His Thought energised and revealed
herself, and stood before Him in the Light-Spark—which is
the Power which existed before the All—which is the perfect
Forethought of the All—the Barbêlô, the Æon perfect in
glory—glorifying Him, because she hath manifested herself
in Him and thinketh Him (*i.e.* gives Him birth). She is the first
Thought, His Image." Barbêlô seems to mean "In the Four is
God": in other words, it is the personified Tetragrammaton
or Great Name commonly rendered by Jehovah.

six Supporters at each gate, in all four and twenty
Supporters, and four and twenty myriads of powers
at each gate, nine Enneads at each gate, ten Decads
at each gate, twelve Dodecads at each gate, and five
Pentads of Powers at each gate. At each gate there
is an Overseer of triple aspect having countenances
Ingenerable, True, and Ineffable. Of these faces
one gazes upon the external æons without the
gate; another beholds Sêtheus, and the third looks
upward to the Sonship contained in every Monad.
There it is that Aphrêdon is discovered with his
twelve Holy Ones and the Forefather, and in that
Space abides also Adam, the Man of the Light, with
his three hundred æons. There also is the Perfect
Mind. All these surround a Basket[9] that knows no
death. The Ineffable face of the Overseer, who
is the Warden of the Holy Place, gazes into the
Holy of Holies upon the Boundless One. Now this
Warden has faces twain. One is disclosed from the
side of the Deep, the other from the side of the
Overseer called the Child (or Servant). For there is

---

[9]   Kanoun. This is a flat, broad basket, originally made of
rush or cane, but often manufactured in precious metals in
later times. It was used in the sacrificial rites of the gods
and was hence classed among sacred things (v. "Basket" in
Hastings' *Ency. of Rel. and Ethics*). What it signifies exactly
I am unable to say. Possibly the rites of the school, if we only
knew them, would throw some light upon the question. The
offerings of bread and wine at the Eucharist may have been
made in the Kanoun. Sometimes in the MS. it seems to be
connected with prayer.

a Deep [within the Holy of Holies] which is named "Light,"[10] or "He who gives the Light," and in this Abyss there is concealed an Alone-begotten Son. He it is who manifests the Three Powers, who is mighty amongst all Powers.

This (? the Holy of Holies) is the Indivisible One, [the atom—Body or Church] that can never be divided, in whom the All is discovered, because all powers are hers.

He who is the Triple Power has three faces, an Aphrêdonian face that is called Aphrêdon Pêxos, in which is found a latent Only-begotten One.

When the (?) Idea comes out of the Deep, Aphrêdon takes the Thought to conduct her to the Alone-begotten of Alone-begottens, to lead her to the Child, so that she may be brought to the Space

---

[10] The Temple of the Plêrômata or Fullnesses seems to be pictured as being in the manner of that in Jerusalem. The Æons of the Inner Space correspond to the Holy of Holies, the Æons of the Middle Space to the Holy Place, and the Æons of the Outer Space to the Court. The various Æons and their powers now described seem to be those of the Inner Space. "Æon" and "Space" are practically equivalent terms, only Æon is on the Mind or Spiritual side of things, Space or Extension (Topos) is on the Life or Body side of things. "Space" is purely the space of mind. It is a Spiritual Body with many members, each of which is a god, having his own individual consciousness and being, and yet partaking perfectly and wholly of a common consciousness or life. Each Æon is a mighty Hierarchy in himself, and his "topos" is a Church or Holy Assembly. The ideal union of these Spaces is in the Monad or Indivisible Point, which is therefore the Church of Churches, the Body of the Man whom no man can comprehend.

of the Triple Power for self-perfecting, and be
escorted in the Space of the Five Ingenerables.

There is also another Space called the Deep,
where there are three Paternities. In the first thereof
is Kaluptô, the Hidden God. In the Second Paternity
there are Five Trees, and in the midst of them an
altar. An Alone-begotten Word stands upon the altar,
having the twelve countenances of the Mind of all
things, and before him are the prayers of all beings
placed. The Universe rejoices over him because he
has manifested himself. He it is that the Invisible
World has struggled to know, and it is on his account
that the Man has appeared. In the Third Paternity
is Silence and the Fount which twelve Anointed
Ones contemplate, beholding themselves therein.
In him are also found Love and the Universal
Mind and furthermore the Universal Mother from
whom has gone forth that Ennead whose names are
Prôtia, Pantia, Pangenia, Loxophania, Loxogenia,
Loxokrateia, Lôia, and Iouêl. She is the First
Beyond Knowledge, the Mother of the Ennead, who
completes a Decad, come forth from the Monad of
the Unknowable.

Following there is another Space, more stretched
out, where is hidden a great treasure which the Universe surrounds. [This Space] is the Immeasurable
Deep where is an altar whereon three Powers are
gathered: a Solitary being, an Unknowable being,
and an Infinite being, in the midst of whom is revealed
a Sonship called the Anointed Glorifier. This is he

who glorifies everyone and impresses upon him the seal of the Father, who brings everybody into the eternity of the First Father who is the One, He for whose sake all is and without whom nothing is. Now this Anointed One has twelve faces, visages Unbounded, Uncontainable, Ineffable, Simple, Imperishable, Solitary, Unknowable, Invincible, Thrice-powerful, Unshakable, Ingenerable, and Pure. These Spaces, where are these twelve founts, named Founts of Reasons, full of eternal life, are called Deeps as well as the Twelve Countenances, because they have received in them all Spaces of Paternity on behalf of the Plêrômata and the Fruit which the Plêrôma emanated, who is Christ who has received the Plêrôma in Himself.

Beyond all these Spaces comes the Deep of Sêtheus. This he who is in them all and is surrounded by twelve Paternities, even in the midst of these is he. Each Paternity has three faces. The first of them is an Indivisible One, and three faces has he, Infinite, Invisible, and Ineffable faces. The Second Father has Uncontainable, Unshakable, and Incorruptible faces. The Third Father has faces Beyond Knowledge, Imperishable, and Aphrêdonian. The Fourth Father has a countenance of Silence, a face of Founts, and a visage Impalpable. The Fifth Father has Solitary, Omnipotent, and Ingenerable faces. The Sixth Father has the face of an All-Father, the face of a Self-Father, and the face of a Fore-father. The Seventh Father has countenances of Universal Mystery, of Universal Wisdom and Universal Origin. Visages has the Eighth Father of Light, Repose, and Resurrection. The Ninth Father has faces Knowable, First Visible, and ... The Tenth Father has Triple-fleshed, Adamic, and Pure faces. The Eleventh Father has faces Triple-powered, Perfect, and Sparkling. The Twelfth Father has a face of Truth, a face of Fore-thought, and a face of After-thought. These are the twelve Paternities which encircle Sêtheus. [Their faces] make in all a [mystic] number thirty six. These are they from whom those of the exterior have received a seal-mark, that is why they glorify them for evermore.[11]

In that Space there are yet twelve other paternities who encircle the head [of Sêtheus] and support a crown there. They dart out rays upon the surrounding worlds by the Grace of the Alone-begotten Word, concealed in him, He that is sought for.

[*The passage enclosed within brackets has been so mutilated by the Coptic scribe that what follows is of the nature of a paraphrase rather than of a*

[11]   Sêtheus and the twelve three-faced Paternities seem to be the paradigms, or heavenly patterns, of the Sun, the signs of the Zodiac, and the thirty-six Decans. He is the Invisible Sun of Righteousness behind the visible flame which measures time. In other words, he is the symbol of the Æon of Æons, the Æon *par excellence*. What time is to the ordinary mundane mind that Sêtheus is to the Alone-begotten and the Monad, whose ineffable union he encompasses. For he is the manifested Sun of Eternity, ⊙. The Monad is the Indivisible Point within the circle or sphere, and the Light-Spark or Logos is within the

translation:—(As to the mysteries of the Word that are so much beyond us, it is not possible to describe them otherwise than as follows. Not possible for us, that is. It is impossible to describe Him as He really is with a tongue of flesh. There are glories too exalted for descriptions moved by thought and for intuition that comes through symbols, except one finds a master who is a kinsman of the deathless race yonder. From such an one can be learned something of the Spaces from whence he came; for he finds the root of all things. The mighty powers of the great æons of the Power that was in Marsanes have said in adoration, "Who is he who hath seen aught in the presence of His Face? "That is because thus does He manifest Himself [? the Alone to the Alone]. Nicotheos has spoken of Him [the Alone-begotten] and seen Him, for he is one of these. He [Nicotheos] said, "The Father exists exalted above all the perfect." Nicotheos has revealed the Invisible and the perfect Triple-power. All perfect men have seen Him, they have declared Him and have given

Point, while Sêtheus himself is, strictly speaking, the circle or sphere, the well-known symbol of Eternity. All the æons are found in the "topos" of Sêtheus, as their divinity is not innate, but comes from conscious participation, hence the name æon. I suggest the name "Sêtheus" is formed from that of the god Sêth, who was a solar deity in some Egyptian traditions. No doubt the differentiation of the name is intentional.

The twelve Paternities about the head are referable to the rays, to the creative powers, the "Divine Imaginings" of the Mystic Sun in their totality.

Him glory with their own lips).]¹² That is the Alone-begotten Word hidden in Sêtheus, He who is called the Dark Ray,¹³ for it is the excess of His light alone that is darkness. Sêtheus reigns by Him.

¹² Schmidt thinks that the name "Nicotheos"—"the Victor God"—is a title of Christ, and that a quotation is given from some lost Apocalypse, called, perhaps, "The Apocalypse of Nicotheos." The whole passage seems to be a definite appeal to the experiences of attained mystics concerning the Dark Ray. The "Perfect" was a technical name, applied to those whose initiation or start had been consummated or perfected. Having been regenerated, they were "gods" or "aeons," conscious of their kinship with the Plêrômata. Each was now a hierarchy in himself, a race, as it were. The passage is probably by a later hand.

¹³ *Cp.* Pseudo Dionysius Myst. Theol.: "The super-unknown, the super-luminous and loftiest height wherein the simple and absolute and unchangeable mysteries are cloaked in the super-lucent darkness of hidden mystic silence, which super-shines most super-brightly in the blackest night, and in the altogether intangible and unseen, superfills the eyeless understanding with super-beautiful brightnesses. And thou, dear Timothy, in thy intent and practice of the mystical contemplations, leave behind both thy senses and thy intellectual operations, and all things known by sense and intellect, and set thyself, as far as may be, to unite thyself in unknowing with Him who is above all being and knowledge; for by being purely free and absolute, out of self and all things, thou shalt be led up to the *Ray of the Divine Darkness*, stripped and loosed of all." The above version is by Dom John Chapman, O.S.B., who says that this passage was "cited throughout the Middle Ages as the *locus classicus* for method of contemplation." This is, except for our text, the earliest mention of the "Dark Ray" in literature. Evidently Pseudo Dionysius did not invent the term himself, but followed a much older Christian tradition. This fact is important for the history of Christian mysticism.

The Alone-begotten holds in His right hand
twelve Paternities, the types of the twelve Apostles,[14]
while in His left hand are thirty Powers. Each of
them emanates twelve two-faced æons after the
type of Sêtheus. One of these faces beholds the
Deep which is in the Interior [of the Temple
of the Plêrôma]; the other looks without upon
the Triple-Power. Each of the Paternities in His
right hand emanates three hundred and sixty-five
powers, according to the word that David spake,
saying, "I will cherish the crown of the year in Thy
Righteousness." For all these Powers encircle the
Alone-begotten Son as a crown, illuminating the
æons with the light of the Alone-begotten, as it is
written, "In Thy light shall we see light." And the
Alone-begotten is lifted up upon [the powers], as
again it is written, "The Chariot of God is a myriad
of multiplications"; and again, "There are millions
of beings who rejoice; the Lord is in them."[15]

This is He who dwells in the Monad in Sêtheus,
which comes from the place concerning which one
does not ask, "Where is it?" She comes from Him who
is before these Fullnesses. From the One and Only,

[14]   This seems to imply a doctrine of pre-existence. Perhaps
the passage is related to John 17:16: "They are not of the
world, even as I am not of the world. . . . As Thou didst send
Me into the world, even so sent I them into the world."

[15]   Cp. Psalm 68:17 (R.V.): "The chariots of God are twenty
thousand, even thousands upon thousands. The Lord is
among them, as in Sinai, in the sanctuary."

even from Him has come forth the Monad, as a ship laden with all good things, or as a full field planted with every manner of tree, or as a city filled with men of every race and with all the statues of the king. Thus it is with the Monad where the Whole is found.

Upon her head twelve Monads form a crown; each has emanated another twelve. Ten Decads encircle her neck, nine Enneads are about her heart, and seven Hebdomads are under her feet, and each has emanated a Hebdomad. The firmament which surrounds her is like a tower with twelve gates, and at every gate are twelve myriads of powers; archangels are they called, or angels. This is the metropolis of the Alone-begotten Son.[16]

Now it is of the Alone-begotten that Phôsilampes[17] has said, "Before all things is He." He it is who has

---

[16]   Further descriptions of this, "the oldest of the Æons," are given later on. From these it will be gathered that the crown is the Crown of Life, and that the twelve gates are also twelve deeps or firmaments, over each of which a Paternity presides. She is called the Indivisible One, either "Point," "Atom," or perhaps even "Body" or "Raiment." As she is both the Spouse and Mother of the Light-Spark within the Æon, I have generally called her the Indivisible Queen.

[17]   Mr Mead suggests that Phôsilampes may be a mystery name of Basilides. Has a commentary on the Gospel of St John been used here, or a commentary on the prologue by Basilides [containing perhaps the teachings of the alleged instructor of Basilides, Glaucias, whose name, rather suggesting the "shining one," may equal "Phôsilampes"], which interpreted "In the beginning" as meaning "In the First Concept or in the Monad was the Word"?

come forth from the Infinite; He who has engendered Himself there and has no seal nor form and has given birth to Himself. This is He who is come forth from the Ineffable One, the Immeasurable One, who truly is, and in whom is found all that truly is, who is the Father Incomprehensible. He is in His Alone-begotten Son, while the All reposes in the Ineffable and Unspeakable King, whom none can move and whose Divinity no one can declare, whose kingdom is not of this world. Meditating upon Him, Phôsilampes has said, "Through Him is That-which-really-is and That-which-really-is-not, through which the Hidden-which-really-is and the Manifest-which-really-is-not exists."

He is the true Alone-begotten God, and all the Fullnesses (Plêrômata) know that it is by Him that they have become gods and that they have become rulers in this name—God. This is He of whom John has said, "In the beginning was the Word, and the Word was in God and the Word was God, and without Him was not anything made. That which was made in Him was Life."

The Alone-begotten is found in the Monad, dwelling in her as in a city, and the Monad is in Sêtheus as a concept, and Sêtheus dwells in the Temple as King and as God. He is the Word creative, who has commanded the Fullnesses to labour; the Creative Mind after the order of God the Father, whom all creation worships as God and Lord, to whom all is subjected.

The Fullnesses wonder at Him [Sêtheus] because of His beauty and grace. Around His head those of the Inner Spaces of the Universe form a crown; those of the external spaces are beneath His feet, while those of the middle spaces encircle Him, all praising Him and saying, "Holy, Holy, Holy, AAA, HHH, EEE, III, OOO, YYY, ΩΩΩ"—that is to say, "Thou art the Living One of Living Ones, Holy of Holies, Being of Beings, Father of Fathers, God of Gods, Lord of Lords, Space of Spaces."[18] They praise Him, saying, "Thou art the House and the Dweller in the House. They praise Him, saying unto the Son concealed in Him, "Thou art: Thou art, O Alone-begotten, Light and Life and Grace."

When Sêtheus sent the Light-Spark from the Indivisible [Body], it burned and gave light to all the Space of the Temple of the Plêrômata. And they, beholding the light of the Spark, rejoiced and uttered myriads and myriads of praises in honour of Sêtheus and of the Light-Spark which was manifested, seeing that in it were all their images,

---

[18]   This repetition of the Seven Vowels gives the following meanings to them:—AAA = Living of Living Ones, HHH = Holy of Holy Ones, EEE = Being of Beings, III = Father of Fatherhoods, OOO = God of Gods, YYY = Lord of Lords, ΩΩΩ = Space of Spaces or Æon of Æons. The High and Holy One, together with His Bride and Mother, the "Universal Church or First Concept," are one in and with the Eternity that they inhabit. Hence "Thou art the House and the Dweller in the House." Time (Æon) and Space (Topos) are here one, or different aspects of the same mode of being.

and they fashioned the Spark among themselves
as a Man light-giving and true. They named Him
"Pantomorphos," and Pure, and Unshakable, and all
the eternities also called him "All-powered." He is
the Servant of the Æons and serves the Fullnesses.[19]
And the Father sealed the Man His Son in their
interior so that they might know Him interiorly, and
the Word moved them to contemplate the Invisible
One beyond knowledge, and they gave glory to this
One and Only One, to the Concept which is in Him
and to the Intelligible Word, praising these Three
who are One, because by Him have they been made
essential beings. The Father took their total image
and made of it a City or a Man and figured in Him
all those of the Plêrôma, that is to say, all the powers.
Each one of them knew his image in the City, for
everyone of the myriads of glories found himself
in the Man or City of the Father which is in the
Plêrôma. The Father took His radiant glory and
made thereof an outer vesture for the Man. . . .

[19] Cp. "The Mind unto Hermes," 16: "The Cosmos is
all-formed [Pantomorphos]—not having forms external
to itself, but changing them, itself within itself"; also the
"Perfect Sermon," xix. 3: "The thirty-six, who have the name
of Horoscopes, are in the self-same space as the fixed stars;
of these the essence chief or Prince is he whom they call
Pantomorph and Omniform, who fashioneth the various forms
for various species." The Pantomorphic Body is the Augoeidês
or Astroeidês, the ray-like or star-like glory (not to be confused
with the "astral body" of modern theosophy). Cp. Origen, Ep.

He created in Him the type of the Temple of the Plêrôma. He made His shoulders, which came out one from the other, after the type of those hundred myriads of powers, less four myriads. He created His fingers and toes like the two Decads, the hidden Decad and the manifest Decad. He created His organ like the Monad concealed in Sêtheus. He created the great reins like Sêtheus. He made His breast like the Interior of the Temple and His feet after the type of the Solitary and Unknowable Ones who serve the Plêrôma, rejoicing with those that rejoice. He made His limbs after the type of the Deep which encloses three hundred and sixty-five Paternities after the type of the Paternities. He fashioned His hair after the type of the Worlds of the Plêrôma and filled Him with wisdom like the Universal Wisdom, and filled Him with interior mystery like Sêtheus and with exterior mystery like the Indivisible [Body]. Incomprehensible

38 ad Pammach: "Another body, a spiritual and ætherial one, is promised us: a body that is not subject to physical touch, nor seen by physical eyes, nor burdened with weight, and which shall be metamorphosed according to the variety of regions in which it shall be. . . . In that spiritual body the whole of us will see, the whole hear, the whole serve as hands, the whole as feet." The Star-body is the body of Resurrection and Ascension. *Cp.* Mark 16:12: "He was manifested in *another form* unto two of them." Also it was the body of "the universal" descent, that which transmitted the Æons from the Plêrôma or Ideal World to the Sensible World, hence it was considered to be "scattered" or in a state of latency, or of mystical death in normal man. To awaken it, to gather it together, or to "raise it

created He Him like the Incomprehensible One, who is in every Space, unique in the Plêrôma. His sides created He after the type of the Four Gates and His two thighs after the type of the Myriarchs who are to the right and left, and His members after the type of those who go forth and those who enter. He created companions surrounding Him after the type of concealed mysteries. . . .

[This was the Man or City that the Plêrômata beheld in the Light-Spark and saw their likenesses therein. They fashioned the Man called Pantomorphos in His likeness, or clothed the Light-Spark in the Star-body.]

The Indivisible Point sent the Light-Spark without the Plêrôma, and [He] descended [as] the Triple-Power into the Spaces of Autogênes, the Self-generated One, and [these Spaces] beheld the grace of the Eternities of Light which had been given unto

from the dead," was one of the first objects of the mystics, who followed the way of the Gnôsis. Its partial resurgence was the first great step in the processes of the Apotheosis. It was the possession of this body, in some degree, which distinguished a man as "spiritual" from the psychic and "hylic" men. The Astroeidês included the "natural" body in its consummation, under a great transmutation, for it was the "Wisdom" at the basis of material nature.

I have transferred the account of the "City of the Man" from where it stands, at the end of the MS., to this place, as it seems more intelligible here, and the exact order has been obscured by the confusion of the leaves.

them, and they rejoiced because that-which-is had come among them.

Then they opened the firmaments and the Light descended below to the lower regions and to those who were without form, having no [true] likeness. It was thus that they got the likeness of the Light for themselves. Some rejoiced because the Light had come to them, and that they had been made rich thereby. Others mourned because they were made poor and that which [they thought] they had was taken away from them. Thus came He, who went forth full of grace, and was taken captive with a captivity.[20] A light of glory was given to the æons who had received the Spark, and guardian spirits were sent to them who are Gamanêl, Etrempsouchos, and Agramas, and those who are with them. They bring help to those who have believed in the Spark of Light.

Now in the Space of the Indivisible Atom are twelve Founts, above which are the twelve Paternities

---

[20] *Cp.* "Pœmandres," 15: " He [the Man], beholding the form like to himself existing in her, in her water, loved it and willed to live in it: and with the will came act, and so he vivified the form devoid of reason. And Nature took the object of her love and wound herself completely round him, and they were intermingled, for they were lovers. . . . Thus, though above the Harmony (or Fate sphere), within the Harmony he [The Man] hath become a slave, . . . and though he is sleepless from a sleepless Sire, yet is he overcome by sleep."

This is the Mystery of the concealment of God in Nature, a mystery that was sometimes presented under the symbol of a self-scattering, sometimes under the symbol of a magical sleep, or mystic death.

who surround the Indivisible [Queen] like Deeps or like Skies and make for Her a crown in which is every kind of life: all modes of Triple-powered life, of Uncontainable life, of Infinite life, of Ineffable life, of Silent life, of Unknown life, of Solitary life, of Unshakable life, of First-manifested life, of Self-born life, of True life. All is therein. Every species is in it, all Gnôses and every power which has received the Light, yea, all Mind manifests itself therein. This is the Crown which the Father of the Universe has placed upon the Indivisible [Queen] with three hundred and sixty-five kinds in it, brilliant and filling the Universe with an incorruptible and unfailing light. This is the Crown which crowns all dominion, the Crown that the Deathless pray for, and by it and in it they will become Invisible Ones [in the world beyond manifestation] on the Day of Joy, who by the Will of the Inscrutable One have from the first been manifested, that is to say, Prôtia, Pantia, Pangenia, and their company. Then shall all the Invisible Eternities receive from Him their crown, so that they may cast themselves among the Invisibles, who shall receive there their crown in the Crown of the Indivisible [Queen], and the Universe shall receive its perfection of incorruption. Because of this it is that those who have taken bodies pray, desiring to abandon the body that they may receive the crown laid up for them in the Incorruptible Eternity.

This is the Indivisible [Queen and Mother], the first æon of all, who has been given all good things by

Him who is above all good things, and she has been given the Immeasurable Deep, wherein are found innumerable Paternities, whereof is the Ennead without seal-mark and having in her the seal-marks of all creatures, and by whom the Ennead emanates twelve Enneads. She [the Indivisible Mother it is] who has in the midst a Space called "The Land productive of Gods," or "The Land which gives birth to the Gods."[21] This is the land of which it has been said, " He who ploughs his soil shall be satisfied with bread and he shall make large his threshing floor," and also, "The Master of the Field, when they shall plough it, shall possess all good things." And all those Powers which are in this land which brought forth the God have received the Crown. That is why they know, because of the Crown upon their heads, if the Inheritors of the Kingdom of Light have [? in truth] been born from the Indivisible Body or not: that is, from Her who is the Universal Mother.[22] She has within Her seven Wisdoms, nine Enneads, ten Decads, and in the midst a great Basket is

[21]   "The Earth that brought forth the God" is the "ground of the individual soul," and is also the Sanctum Sanctorum of the Universe, the Hidden Sanctuary where the "Man" is raised from mystical death or is reborn. No doubt the symbolism is drawn from Egyptian sources.

[22]   This passage might be paraphrased, "Those who have received Life and Light in the Concealed Sanctuary of the Soul know, through this Crown of Perfection, that the Inheritors of the Kingdom of Light are indeed reborn from the Indivisible Body, who is the Mother of us all.

revealed. A mighty Invisible [Hierarch] stands above it with a mighty Ingenerable [Hierarch] and a mighty Unbounded [Hierarch], each one triple-countenanced, and the prayer, the blessing, and the hymn of creatures are given place in this Basket which is in the midst of the Universal Mother, in the midst of the seven Wisdoms, in the midst of the nine Enneads, and in the midst of the ten Decads. For all these [creatures] stand upright in the Basket, made perfect by the Fruit of the Æons, He who has been ordained for them by the Alone-begotten concealed in the Indivisible [Atom]. He [the Fruit of the Æons] has a Fount before Him surrounded by twelve Holy Ones, each one wearing a Crown on his head and having twelve powers, who surround Him within, praising the Alone-begotten king and crying, "It is because of Thee that we ray forth glory, and it is by Thee that we behold the Father of the Universe, AAA, ΩΩΩ,[23] and the Mother of all the good, She who is hidden in every space"—that is to say, the contriving thought (Epinoia) of all the Eternities, the conceiving thought of all gods and of all lords— "She is the Gnôsis of all the Unseen beings, and Thy Image is the Mother of all the Boundless Ones, the Power of all the Infinites."

---

[23]   AAA ΩΩΩ = The Living Space of Spaces, Æon of Æons. See note 18 and *cp*. Rev. 1:8, 17-18: " I am Alpha and Omega . . . the First and the Last, and the Living One; and I was dead, and, behold, I am alive unto the æon of æons."

Praising the Alone-begotten, they cry, "It is because of Thy Image[24] that we have seen Thee, that we have run to Thee, that we have clung to Thee, that we have received the Incorruptible Crown which is known through Her. Glory be to Thee, O Alone-begotten, for ever and ever."

Then together do they all say Amen.

For [? Jesus, the Fruit of the Æons] became a Body of Light, He crossed the Æons of the Indivisible [Body] until He came to the Alone-begotten who is in the Monad and who dwells in Peace and Solitude. He received the Grace of the Alone-begotten—that is to say, His Christhood or His Perfecting. Also He received the Eternal Crown. He is the Father of all Light-Sparks, the chief of all Immortal bodies, and this is He for whose sake resurrection is given to the body.[25]

---

[24]   The Body of Christ, which in its transcendental aspect is also His Bride and Mother. *Cp.* 2 Clem. xiv: " I do not suppose that you know not that the living Church is the body of Christ; for the scripture saith, 'God made Man, male and female; the male is Christ, the female the Church; and the books and the Apostles belong not to the Church that now is, but to the Church which is from above. For it is spiritual, as is our Jesus, but is manifested in these last days to save us. But the Church, being spiritual, is manifested in the flesh of Christ. . . . Great is the Life and Immortality which this flesh can partake of—that is, of the Holy Spirit which is joined to it—nor can any declare or utter what the Lord has prepared for His chosen."

[25]   This extremely interesting and important passage is also one of great difficulty, for it is full of technical terms

But besides the Indivisible Queen and besides her Ennead without seal-mark, in which is found all seal-marks, there are three other Enneads, of which each emanates nine Enneads. In the first of these is revealed a Basket round which three Fathers are gathered: an Infinite Father, an Ineffable Father, and an Uncontainable Father. In the middle of the second Ennead is a Basket, and three Fathers are there: an Invisible Father, an Ingenerable Father, and an Unshakable Father. In the third Ennead is also revealed a Basket which encloses three Paternities: a Solitary Father, an Unknown Father, and a Triple-Powered Father. It is through these that the Universe has known God. They ran towards Him and have engendered an innumerable multitude of æons, and in each Ennead they offered myriads and myriads of praises.

and allusions which would need a small treatise to elucidate properly. For example, it seems to imply the doctrine of two Logoi that Clement of Alexandria was accused of teaching, and which is found in certain Hellenistic writings. The "Body of Light" is the Astroeidês in which the "Adept" can cross the "Fate-Sphere," the "Midst," the regions of consciousness where mechanical cause and effect prevail and contact the Plêrôma, or Universe of Divine Freedom and Fullness. "Charts" or "Grace" is the name of the Bride or Body of the Logos, and the use of it here symbolises a "raiment" or "Body" still more exalted than the Astroeidês. It is the Body beyond the Stars, the Monadic Robe or "Robe of Glory," into which the "Star-like Body" was transformed at the Horos, Limit or Boundary of the Worlds of Difference and of Sameness. What

In each of these Enneads there is a Monad, and in each Monad a Space called "Incorruptible": that is to say, "Holy ground." There is a Fount in the ground of each of these Monads, and myriads and myriads of Powers who have received on their heads a crown of the Crown of the Triple-Power. In the middle of these Enneads and of these Monads is an immeasurable Deep towards which all the Universe looks, those that are internal as well as those that are external, having above it twelve Paternities, each surrounded by thirty Powers.

The First Paternity is a face of the Infinite One, and thirty infinite powers surround him.

The Second Paternity is a face of the Invisible One, and thirty invisible powers surround him.

The Third Paternity is a face of the Uncontainable One, and thirty uncontainable powers surround him.

The Fourth Paternity is a face of the Invincible One, and thirty invincible powers surround him.

The Fifth Paternity is a face of the All-powerful One, and thirty all-powerful powers surround him.

kind of Peace was that in which the Alone-begotten dwelt in the Monad? A Peace most truly given to those within and those without, for in it all things were created. To realise what is meant we must remember that "Charis" and "Resurrection "were names of "Staurus," the Pillar that made with Horos the Great Cross referred to more than once. "Peace," then, was the state of the Logos in Mystic crucifixion, the Peace of God which established, reconciled, justified all things. Hence it can be inferred what transformation the Star Body had to undergo

The Sixth Paternity is a face of the All-Wise One, and thirty all-wise powers surround him.

The Seventh Paternity is a face of the Unknown One, and thirty unknown powers surround him.

The Eighth Paternity is a face of the Solitary One, and thirty solitary powers surround him.

The Ninth Paternity is a face of the Ingenerable One, and thirty ingenerable powers surround him.

The Tenth Paternity is a face of the Unshakable One, and thirty unshakable powers surround him.

The Eleventh Paternity is a face of the Universal Mystery, and thirty universal mysteries surround him.

The Twelfth Paternity is a face of the Triple-Powered One, and thirty triple-powers surround him.

And in the midst of the Immeasurable Deep there are five Powers which are called by these inef-fable names :

The first is called Love, and from her comes all love.

to become the Robe of Glory. The Cross and the Master were one. The Cross of Calvary was to the Gnôstic Teacher the outer and efficacious sign of this Mystery or Sacrament. So also the Pentecostal outpouring recorded in Acts was the outward sign, or sacramental token, of the assumption by the Master of the Robe of Glory, the vesture of the Monad or Transcendental and Universal Church, which could not be assumed here. From thenceforth the band of disciples became a Church, the Mystic Body of Christ, the outward sign of concealed mysteries; and it

The second is called Hope, and it is by her that we hope in the Alone-begotten, the Son of God.

The third is called Faith, and it is by her that we believe the mysteries of the Ineffable One.

The fourth is called Gnôsis, and it is by her that we know the First Father, Him because of whom we live that we may know Him. [Gnôsis] the Mystery of Silence, who spake before all things, that which is hidden, the First Monad, for whom the Universe became being. It is upon the head of this Mystery that the three hundred and sixty-five substances form a crown like the hair of human kind, and the Temple of the Plêrôma is as a stairway beneath her feet. This is the Gate of God.[26]

The fifth is called Peace, and it is by her that we give Peace to all, to those within and to those without,

---

will be seen in what manner Jesus was the Father of all Light-Sparks and gave resurrection to the body. Such was the teaching of the Gnôsis. To make the matter clear to readers interested in mysticism, but unfamiliar with Hellenistic technical terms, it may be said that the "Bodies" so often referred to may be taken as standing for what may be called the Life side of various stages of mystical consciousness, as "Light" stands for the Mind side; but Life and Light are one.

[26] "The Gate of God." Cp. the Naasene Document in Hippolytus: "This Mystery is the Gate of Heaven, and this is the House of God, where the Good God dwells alone; into which no impure man shall come, no psychic, nor fleshly man, . . . but it is kept under watch for the Spiritual alone—where, when they come, they must cast away their garments, and all become bridegrooms, obtaining their true manhood through the Virginal Spirit. For this is the Virgin big with child,

for it is in her that all things have been created.

This is that Abyss Immeasurable in which is found three hundred and sixty-five Paternities, thanks to whom they have devised the year.

This is the Abyss which surrounds the Temple of the Plêrôma, where is revealed the Triple-Power with his branches and his trees, and Mousanios and those which belong to him. There also is Aphrêdon and his twelve Holy Ones, and a Basket is in the midst of them. They come to carry in it the praises, the hymns, the prayers and supplications of the Mother of the Universe, the Mother of the (manifested?) worlds who is called Phanerios,[27] and to give them a form, thanks to the twelve Holy Ones. They send them into the Plêrôma of Sêtheus, by which act they call to mind those of the external world in which there is matter.

conceiving and bearing a Son—not psychic, not fleshly, but a blessed Æon of Æons."

"Gnôsis," then, was the Mystery of Regeneration or Rebirth from above. It will be observed that the text shows no hostility to "Faith." This is an indication of early date. "Mystery" is often, though not always, the equivalent to "Sacrament."

[27] There is then another "Universal Mother," Phanerios or Phaneia (= "Wisdom without the Plêrôma"). In the last resort the two Mothers are one. Phaneia is the Mother of the manifested world in which there is matter, but she does not seem to be in exile, as in the Sophia Myth. Like Isis in the Osiris legend, she seems to have gone forth to gather together the self-scattered limbs of the Man and to redeem Him from captivity through the efforts of the great hierarchs that are given to her.

This is the Deep where the Triple-Power rayed out the splendours of His glory, after He had been to the Indivisible Mother and had received the Grace of the One Beyond Knowledge, by which He had gotten such a Sonship that the Fullnesses were not able to stand upright before Him because of the excess of His light and brilliancy thereof. The whole Plêrôma was troubled, the Abyss and all it contained was moved, and the [æons] fled to the world of the Mother [Phanerios], and the Mystery ordained that the veils of the æons should be drawn until the Overseer had established them once more. And the Overseer established the æons once more, as it is written, "He has established the Earth, and it shall not be moved," and again, "The Earth has been dissolved and all that therein is."[28]

Then the Triple-Power went forth: the Son was concealed in him, and the crown of confirmation was upon his head, making myriads and myriads of glories. They cried, "Make straight the way of the Lord and receive the grace of God: every æon

---

[28]   The pre-existence of the soul is taught, also the loss of the memory of its true nature owing to its fall into "Matter" [Hyle]. But this fall is not regarded as either a sin or a mistake, but as a needful step in the mystery of Rebirth or "Re-ordering." The Overseer is the "Mind of all Masterhood," the Logos, the Second Father of all.

It is tempting to connect the Triple-Power with the Triple-Bodied Man of the Naasene Document and see in him the symbol of a simple Universal Consciousness "polarised" into the three states of Spiritual, Psychic, and Material.

which is empty shall be filled with the grace of the Alone-begotten Son."

The Father holy and all-perfect stood above the Deep Immeasurable. It is in Him that all perfection is found, and in His fullness have we received grace. Then the world was established; it ceased to shake; the Father fashioned it so that it might nevermore be shaken, and the æon of the Mother remained full of those that were in it until the ordering came from the Mystery concealed in the First Father, He from whence came the Mystery; when His Son re-established the Universe once more in His Gnôsis, that which re-enforms the Universe.

Then Sêtheus sent the Logos Dêmiourgos, having with him a multitude of Powers, wearing the crowns on their heads; and their crowns darted forth rays. The brilliancy of their bodies is as the life of the Space into which they are come; the word that comes out of their mouths is life Æonian, and the light that comes from their eyes is a rest for them; the movement of their hands is their flight to the place from whence they have come, and their gazing on their own faces is Gnôsis of their interior nature; their going towards them is their return once more within; the stretching forth of their hands establishes them; the hearing of their ears is the intuition in their hearts; the union of their limbs is the regathering of the dispersal of Israel; their self-understanding is their contemplation of the Logos; the writing upon their fingers is the number which has gone forth, even as it is written, "He counteth the number of the Stars and calleth them all by their names."

And the whole union was made by the Logos Dêmiourgos with those who had come out of the turmoil that had been: altogether they became one and the same body, as it has been written, "They have all become one and the same body in this One and Only One." Then this Logos Dêmiourgos became a mighty God, Lord, Saviour, Christ, King, the Good, Father, Mother. This is He whose work was good: He was glorified and became Father to those that believed: He became Law in Aphrêdonia and mighty.

Then went forth Pandêlos [All-manifest]; she had a crown on her head, and she placed it upon them who had believed.[29]

The Power of the Æons [? the Indivisible Queen, the Mother within the Plêrôma] ordered the Hierarchy of the World of the Virgin Mother [Phaneia, the Mother without the Plêrôma, she who brings into manifestation] according to the Order of the Inner Space. She placed in it the Light-Spark after the pattern of the Monad and placed therein the concealment which surrounds Him. She ordained the Propator after the Order of the

[29]   This Vision of the Advent of the Creative Word seems to be in part a summary and anticipation of things described otherwise later in the MS. After it the writer (or writers) goes back and describes the " Re-ordering" from the time that "the veils of the æons were drawn" from various points of view. Various Cosmic processes are delineated symbolically, and their simultaneous working is not excluded.

Indivisible Body and the twelve Holy Ones which surround it, having crowns on their heads and seals of glory in their right hands, after the type found in the Indivisible Point. In the midst of these is Love; a face of the Triple-Power is in the Fount, and there is a Basket which twelve Paternities surround, in whom a Sonship is concealed.

She ordained the Autopatôr according to the order of the Ennead without seal-mark and gave him authority over all that is only self-fathered, and gave him a crown of all-glory and love, and Peace, Truth, and myriads of powers, so that he might gather together those who had been dispersed by the troubling which had taken place when the [Light-Spark] went forth with joy. As for the Prince of the Universe, he who has the triple-power to make alive and to destroy, she ordained the Son Prôtogennêtôr after the order of the Triple-Power. She gave him a ninefold Ennead and five tenfold Decads, and that he might have power to accomplish the warfare imposed upon him, she gave him the first-fruits of the Sonship concealed in her that he might be able to become a Triple-Power. He received the Vow of the Sonship because the Universe[30] had been sold [? into slavery], and took upon him the warfare entrusted to him and made arise all that was pure in matter. A world made he, an æon, a town; the world

---

[30] The Universal Man had fallen into bondage in the Fate-Sphere.

which is called "Incorruptibility" and "Jerusalem."
It is also called "The New Earth," and "Self-
Perfect," and "Without King." This earth is an earth
that brings forth gods, a life-giving earth indeed.
This is the earth that the Mother (? Phaneia) asked
to have established. That is why she (? the Mother
Above) has placed orders or hierarchy in this earth
and has placed in it Providence and Love. This is
the earth of which it has been written, "The earth
which drank the rain a multitude of times": that is to
say, which has multiplied the light in her multitudes
and multitudes of times, since the (light) went forth
until its return; that is to say, it is that from which
the Man is named "Sensible." He is fashioned,
He has been created according to the type of
this earth, He who has been saved from His Self-
dispersion by the Prôtogennêtôr.[31] Because of that,
the Father of all those of the Universe, He who has
no [bridal] bed has sent [Him, ? the Man] a crown

[31]   I think that what we are to understand is, that the Man is
raised from His state of Mystical Death or Self-dispersion by the
Prôtogennêtôr (Son, First Parent), crowned with the Lights of
Wisdom by the Hidden Father "Who has no consort," and robed
with cosmic life by the Mother. Compare what has already been
said about the Robe of Glory and the outward signs of its descent
at Pentecost. The work of the Mantle would seem to symbolise
the re-ordering work of the Church, the "New Creation," the
new impulse on its mystical side. Is Prôtogennêtôr, then, a
cryptic title of Christ? In a sense I think it is, but there are other
issues which are better discussed at a later point.

    The Title "Without King" recalls the Naasene Document
and its "One is the Race without a King which is born Above."

bearing the names of all those of the Universe, whether Infinite or Ineffable, or Uncontainable, or Incorruptible, or Unknown, or Solitary, or All-powerful, or Indivisible. This is the crown of which it is written, "They gave it unto Solomon on the day of his exultation of heart."

The First Monad sent Him [the Man] an ineffable vesture which is all Light, all Life, all Love, all Hope, all Faith, all Wisdom, all Gnôsis, all Truth, all Peace, all Witness, all Universal Mother, all Universal Mystery, all Fount, all Universal Perfection, all Invisible, all Unknown, all Infinite, all Ineffable, all Abyss, all Uncontainable, all Fullness, all Silence, all Unshakable, all Unengendered, all Universal Solitary, all Monad, all Ennead, all Dodecad, all Ogdoad, all Decad, all Hebdomad, all Hexad, all Pentad, all Tetrad, all Triad, all Dyad, all Monad. The whole Universe is in it, and the Universe has found itself therein and knows itself therein.† It gave light to all in its ineffable light, and it was given myriads and myriads of powers, so that the Universe might be established once and for all. It gathered together its skirts and gave them the form of a veil which surrounded it [the Universe] on every side. It poured itself over all things, raised them up and divided them according to the Hierarchies, according to the orders, and according to Providence. Then that-which-was separated itself

† See n. 29.

from that-which-was-not, and that-which-was-not
was the evil manifested in matter; and the Robe of
Power severed that-which-was from that-which-
was-not. That-which-was it called Æonian, and
that-which-was-not it called Hyle (matter). It
separated by the Midst that-which-was from that-
which-was-not, and placed veils between these
twain. It placed purifying powers, so that they might
purge them and make them clean. It gave in this
manner an order to that-which-is and made of the
Mother the chief. It gave it ten æons, and each æon
has a myriad powers; there is also a Monad and an
Ennead in each æon.

The [Robe of Power] placed in her [? Phaneia]
an Universal Motherhood and therewith a Power that
had hitherto been concealed therein, so that none
knew thereof. [? The Robe] placed a great Basket,
above which stand three Powers, an Ingenerable One,
an Unshakable One, and the Great Pure One. It gave
to [? the world order] the twelve other Powers who
have received the crown and who surround it. It gave
it also the Seven Stratelatai,[32] who have the seal of the
All-completing [Panteleios], and have on their heads
crowns in which there are twelve stones of Adamant,
which come from Adam, the Man of Light.

[The Robe of Power] established the Propatôr in
all the æons of the Mother of [the Manifestation] of

---

[32]   The Seven Stratelatai, leaders or generals, are perhaps
the seven Planets.

all things, and gave him the full power of Paternity, and Powers to obey him as Father and as First Father of all that exists. It placed upon his head a crown of twelve kinds; it gave him a Power which is Triple-powered and All-powered; it gave him Sonship and myriads and myriads of Glories. It turned the Plêrôma towards him and gave him power to make live and to destroy. It gave him a power of the æons so that he might manifest it, with the myriads and myriads of out-rayed Glories, like the other æons that were with him. The Power which has been given to the Propatôr is called Prôtophanes, because he is the first to be manifested, and Agennêtos, because no one has engendered him. Also Ineffable and "Without Name" is he called, and also Autogênes and Autothelêtos, because he has manifested himself by his own will. Yet again is he named Autoloxastos, for he manifested himself with the Glories that were his. Yet again is he termed Invisible, for he is hidden and none can see him.

Now [the Robe of Power] gave unto the Propatôr another Power, that which since the beginning has caused the Light-Spark to appear in this Space, and who is named with names Holy and All-perfecting. Who is Prôtia, that is to say, the First, and is also called Pantia—she who is found in all—and Pangenia—she who has brought forth all in the world—and Loxogenia—she who has brought Glory to birth—and Loxophania—Manifester of Glory—and Loxokrateia—she who has dominion over Glory—and Arsenogenia—she who brings forth males—and Lôia—of which the interpretation is God with us—and Jouêl—of which the interpretation is God for ever—she it is who has ordained that these Powers should appear whose name is called Phaneia, of which the translation is Manifestation. The angel who has appeared with them is he whom the Glories name Loxogenes and Loxophanes, of which the interpretation is "He who engenders Glory" and "He who manifests Glory," for he is one of those Glories who stand about that mighty power called Loxokrator, because in his manifestation he has had dominion over the great Glories.

Such are the Powers that were given to the Propatôr when he was placed in the æon of the Mother, and myriads and myriads of Glories, Angels, Archangels, and Liturgies were bestowed upon him, so that they might serve him, those of matter. They gave him power over everything. He made for himself a mighty æon and placed therein a mighty Plêrôma and a great temple and all the Powers that he had taken and placed within himself, and he rejoiced with them, bringing forth his creatures again according to the commandment of the Father hidden in the Silence, Who had sent him these riches; and the Crown of Fatherhood was given to him because he had been made the Father of all those who came after him. Then he cried out and said, "My children, with whom I travail again until Christ be formed in you";

and again he cried, "Yea, I would set beside a holy virgin an only husband, Christ."

But when he had seen the Grace that the Father in secret had given unto him (that is Himself a Propatôr), he wished to turn the Universe to the Father in secret, for it is His will that the Universe should turn to Him. And when the Mother saw all the grandeurs which had been given unto her Propatôr, she rejoiced greatly, she exulted; that is why she said, "My heart has rejoiced and my tongue has been in exultation." Then she cried to the Power Infinite who stands hard by the æon of the Father, that mighty Power of Glory that the Glories call Trigenielos,[33] that is to say, Three Engendered, and who is named also Trigenes and also Harmes. She prayed also unto Him who is concealed in every Space that He would send him the Mother of Him who has withdrawn Himself. The Father in secret sent him the Mystery who reclothes all the æons like the Glories who form the Crown Pantelês, that is to say, of Perfection, so that he [the Propatôr] might place the Crown upon the head of the Indivisible [Body] hidden within her, Incorruptible and Unengendered. With [her He sent] the mighty Power which is in her company, she

---

[33]   *Cp.* the Akhmim Codex: "She (Barbêlô) is the First Thought, his Image, she becometh the First Man; that is the Virginal Spirit, she of the triple Manhood, the triple-powered one, the triple-named, triple-born, the æon which ages not, the Man-woman."

who is called Arsenogenia, who replenishes all the æons of Glory. Thus from him shall the Universe receive the Crown.

Then she established the Autopatôr Father and Æonian One; and gave unto him the æon of the Concealed One in which are found all things, such as species, faces, images, forms, questions, dissemblances, and changes, that which counts and that which is counted, that which thinks and that which is thought. She made a vesture thereof over all which is in him, so that he might give to him who asked him. She gave unto him ten Powers, and nine Enneads, five Æons, and she gave unto him Light; and that gave him power over all secret things, so that he might show mercy to those who had fought, who had towards the æon fled from matter, leaving it behind them. They have fled to the æon of the Autopatôr; they have made their own the promise which has been promised by Him who said, "He who forsakes father, mother, brother, sister, wife, children, and riches, and takes up his cross and follows Me, shall receive the promises that I have promised unto him, and I will give unto them the Mystery of the Father in Secret, because they have loved that which was truly theirs and have fled from him who pursues them with injustice." And he [Autopatôr] gave them Glory, Joy, Exaltation, Jubilation, Peace, Hope, Faith, Love, and the Truth which changes not. This is the Ennead with which he rewarded those that fled from matter;

they became happy, they became perfect, they knew God and the Truth, they comprehended the Mystery which works in the Man; for what cause He has revealed Himself, that they might see Him, for He is in truth Invisible; and for their sakes He has revealed in words His Logos, so that they might know Him and become gods and perfect.

When the Mother established the Prôtogennêtôr as her son, she gave unto him the Power of the Sonship; she gave unto him armies of Angels and Archangels; she gave unto him twelve Powers who served him; she gave unto him a robe to consummate all things in him, for in it is revealed every kind of body: the body of fire, the body of water, the body of air [? spirit], the body of earth, the body of wind, the body angelic, the body archangelic, the body of Powers, the body of Dominions, the body of Gods, the body of Lords—in a word, every kind of body, so that nothing might hinder him from mounting into the heights or descending into the depths of Noun. This is the Prôtogennêtôr to whom those of the internal and external Spaces have promised all things that please him, and it is he who separates all matter; for he brooded over it like a bird who stretches her wings over her eggs. Even thus did the Prôtogennêtôr unto matter, and made myriads and myriads of species and kinds come forth. When Matter was warmed she produced the multitudes of Powers that were in her, and he separated them into species and kinds. He gave them a law to love one another, to honour God and to praise Him, and to seek

for Him, who He is and what He is, and to wonder at
the place from whence they had come forth, so narrow
and so sad, and not to return thither again, but to
follow him who had given them a law and made them
come out of the darkness of Matter, their Mother. He
had said to them, "Let there be light." For they did not
know if there were such a thing as light or not. Then
he gave them the command not to hurt one another,
and left them to go to the Space of the Mother of the
Universe beside the Propatôr and the Autopatôr, so
that together they might draw up those who had come
forth from matter.

Then the Mother of the Universe,[34] the Propatôr,

---

[34]   Who are the Mother and the three great hierarchs? It is
tempting to connect the three with the three traditional paths
of Purgation, Illumination and Union, Water, Fire and Spirit.
The Propatôr, who desires to turn the World to God, and who is,
through the descent of a particular power, the Father-Mother
of the Spiritual Life to come, may symbolise the process of
Purgation and the Baptism of Water; the Autopatôr, who utters
the promises of Christ and who has the power of an Ennead of
initiation, may typify the Illuminative Life and the Baptism of
Fire; while the Prôtogennêtôr, robed in cosmic consciousness,
so that he can walk even the waters of the Primal Deep (Noun),
who draws forth finally from the material life, may represent the
inception of the Life of Union and the Baptism of the Spirit. All
this may be true, but, if I mistake not, there is more behind the
veil of symbolism, and it is continual allusions to this *more*, plain
enough to the person for whom it was intended, that renders the
MS. so peculiarly difficult. Who is Phaneia, the Mother without
the Plêrôma, who owes her position to the descent of the Royal
Robe? She stands for nature in what may be called its sacramental
aspect, and she also stands for the Churches, if I mistake not,

the Autopatôr, the Prôtogennêtôr, and the Powers of
the æon of the Mother sang a great hymn to the One
and Only God, praising Him and saying:

"Thou alone art Boundless, Thou only art the
Deep, Thou only art the Incomprehensible One, for
Thou art He whom all beings seek and [without Thy
grace] find Thee not, for none can know Thee against
Thy will, and none can praise Thee against Thy will.
For Thy will only is a Space for Thee, for nothing can
contain Thee who art the Space for all. Thee I pray
that Thou mayest give an holy ordering to those of
the World, that Thou mayest dispose my offspring
according to Thy will. Grieve not my offspring, for

and more particularly for the community or order to which the
writer or writers belonged. This implies a certain claim to a high
mystical self-knowledge on the part of that community. Again,
the title "Son Prôtogennêtôr" is most significant. He that bore it
must be the Son of the Sacred House, the "Son of the Doctrine,"
and the First Parent, or Father in God, of those to come after.
He invites comparison not only with the Saviour of the Gospels,
but also with figures that appear in the myths of the mystery
cults: with Horos, the son of Isis, with Hermes the Thrice-
Great, with the "Eagle" or "Father" whose title represented the
highest grade of the Mithriaca. I suggest that he may represent
the ideal candidate in the mystery of initiation—that is to say, he
who, by entering into himself, has attained to the "unio mystica,"
has raised up the "Man" within himself, has been "reborn" as a
god in Divine consciousness, and so is qualified to hand on the
vital processes of the Gnôsis to others, becoming thereby their
spiritual parent. So he is called Son Prôtogennêtor. He is Christ
in the sense that Galahad of the "Quest," and Parsifal of Wagner's
great drama are Christ. The theory of initiation as conceived in
the early mystical communities seems, in part at any rate, to rest

never has anything been grieved by Thee; yet no
one knows Thy Counsel. Of Thee all beings of the
Inner and the Outer Worlds have need, Thou only
Incomprehensible, Thou only beyond All vision,
beyond All mind. Thou only hast given character to
all creatures and hast manifested them in Thyself. Of
that which is not yet manifested art Thou the Creator,
upon the proposition that he who has himself attained to Union
with God is able to "start," to "initiate," in suitable persons,
and under certain conditions, those processes which, under
Providence, result in a like consummation. Thus we appear to
have a claim in the MS. to a transmitted "Mastership" in the
ranks of the order going back to Jesus Himself: "For whose sake
resurrection is given to the body. He is the Father of all Light-
Sparks." The Propatôr and Autopatôr would seem to represent
different aspects of this claim. "Gnôsis" was not the possession
of a body of secret Doctrine in the sense of having a number of
formal propositions containing occult information, but a vital
knowledge of the processes of "Regeneration" or "Apotheosis."
   Then, again, we have the idea of a "Divine Mind" or
"Logos" manifesting Himself through a Body of Universal
Consciousness, represented sacramentally (that is to say effectually) in the "physical world" by the bodies of a body of believers.
The rites of this body symbolised, again "effectually," the modes
and activities of the Body of Universal Consciousness of which it
was the outward sign, just as its doctrines reflected on the plane
of mentation and discourse the workings of the Divine Mind,
which are above mentation and discourse, though not contrary
to it. The acceptance of these ideas seems to have constituted
"Pistis"—"the Faith by which we believe in the Mysteries of
the Man"—a mode of the Divine Energy which resulted in
good works. "Gnôsis" was the knowledge of the processes
by which these ideas passed from the life of formal belief and
intellectual assent into the life of realised consciousness. The
"Hylics," men in Hyle or "Matter," were "the children of this

and Thou alone dost know these things, for we know them not [of ourselves]. Thou alone revealest them unto us [through Symbols and Images], so that we may supplicate Thee on their behalf, so that Thou mayest make them manifest, and we may know them [as they are in themselves apart from all Symbols] by Thy Grace alone. Thou alone hast raised up the

world," so absorbed in the life of the senses five that they lived like "brute beasts without understanding." [Hyle as a technical term was not always understood too literally by the Gnôstics and Platonists (see various passages in Codex Bruce), but derived its importance as the symbol of a certain state of consciousness.] "Psychics" were those whose consciousness was sufficiently aroused to accept a formal belief in viewless Divine Energies and to order their social conduct on the basis of that belief. The "Spiritual," the "Perfect," those perfected in Gnôsis, that is, were those that were actually conscious of participating in a Mind in common and in a Body of transcendental energy in common. This Mind (Logos), Light-Spark, and Body (Monad) constituted a sole Being, Man, or the Son of Man, neither male nor female, and yet both, who enveloped all things, even those of Hyle (v. the Naasene Document) in His Infinite Perfections, who manifested all things, who was concealed in all things and who was above all things. An ideal Church or Community of "Spiritual" men, conscious of the whole Man in each of its members, could focus within itself, without any robbery, all the energies of the Universe, and by concentrating and applying them in a certain manner could give birth to the whole order within the consciousness of the called and chosen candidate, who thus became a "Self-Knowing," "Self-Fathered," "Fore-Fathered" god, a "Race without a King in the name God." His substance was "enformed" by the Sacraments of the Manifested Order (Phaneia), and the substance thus "enformed" was finally "assumed," "translated," "transformed," what you will, in a mode utterly beyond all symbol and image by the "descent"

Secret Worlds to Thyself, so that they might know
Thee, for Thou hast given unto them the boon of
knowing Thee, for Thou hast given birth unto them
from Thy Incorporeal Body and hast taught them
that from Thy Self-productive Mind Thou hast the
Man brought forth in Contemplation and in a perfect
Concept, yea, even the Man brought forth by Mind
to whom Contemplation has given a form. Thou it is
who hast bestowed all good things upon the Man, and
He weareth them like vestures. He putteth them on
like garments and wrappeth Himself with Creation as

of the Divine "Grace," "First Concept," "Ennead and Monad
Without Seal-Mark," "Barbêlô" (again what you will), and given
final "Re-birth in the Light of the Mind." To form an Ideal
community of this kind, a community of gods in God, by a series
of grades or steps, places of "Repentance" or "change" slowly
taken, was, I believe, the purpose of those responsible for the
original of the present MS. "They began from the base upwards
that the building might unite them to their companions"—souls
that in æonian bliss beheld the Face of God unveiled. Into this
building plan the Neophyte was initiated to give thereto his soul
and body as a willing oblation and sacrifice. It seems a reasonable
suggestion to offer that this document consists of a series of
meditations and spiritual exercises given to the candidate before
one of the inner "initiations" or sacramental "starts" that was
consummated beyond the veil of signs and symbols. For such
an end not only Faith, not only a reasonable Foundation in an
accepted philosophy, that of Plato, but an Imagination intensified
into intuition was needed. Hence these strange hieroglyphs on
the expressed veil. The Child of Fire must behold rising within
himself from the Immeasurable Abyss of Godhead the five-rayed
morning star of Love, Faith, Hope, Gnôsis, and Peace, the herald
of the Perfect Dawn of a New Birth.
    Possibly "Propatôr," "Autopatôr" and "Prôtogennêtôr"

with a robe.[35] This Man is He whom all the Universe yearneth to know, for Thou alone it is who hast ordained unto the Man to manifest Himself, so that in Him Thou mightest be known and that all might learn that it is Thou who hast brought Him forth and that Thou art manifested according to Thy Will.

"Thee do I invoke, and I pray Thee, O Father of all Fatherhood, Lord of all Lords, to give an holy ordering unto my kinds and to my offspring, that I may rejoice in Thy Name and in Thy goodness, O Thou Sole King, O Thou who changest not. Bestow upon me from Thy goodness, and I will make known unto my children that Thou art their Saviour."[36]

When the Mother had finished praying to the Boundless One Beyond Knowledge, who fills the whole Universe and gives life unto all, He heard her and those with her, for all of them were His own, and He sent unto her a Power who came forth from the Man whom they desired to behold.

may also have been the official designations of hierophants in the sacramental side of some "Mystery" consummated in solitude, from which the candidate returned an "Epopt."

[35] Cp. Ps. 104:1, 2: "Thou art clothed with honour and majesty: who coverest thyself with light as with a garment."

[36] This hymn or prayer seems to be an invocation to the "Dark Ray" on behalf of the candidate (and also for the building up of the "Ideal Order"). The consummation, beyond all signs and images, is in the hands of God alone. A "start" may be effected by duly qualified hierophants under certain conditions, but the crown "Pantêlos" is given by the "Father of all Fatherhood" alone.

From Being Unbounded came forth the Infinite
Spark of Light, at whom all the æons wondered,
asking themselves where He had been concealed
before manifesting Himself from the Infinite Father,
He from whom the Universe was manifested and who
was latent therein. The Powers of the Secret Worlds
followed Him when they were manifested and came
into the Temple of the Plêrôma. He hid Himself
amidst the Powers who came forth from the Father
in Secret.[37] He made a world and bore it into the
Temple. Then the Powers of the Plêrôma beheld Him
and loved Him and praised Him in hymns ineffable,
unspeakable to tongues of mortal flesh, and good to
dream of in the heart of man. He received their hymn
and made a veil surrounding their world like a wall;
then went He to the borders of the Universal Mother
[without] and stood above the Universal Æon.[38] The

[37] This looks as if in this system the Fruit of the Plêrôma
was also the Father of the Fullnesses. The phrase "He made
a world and bore it into the Temple" seems to mean that He
assumed a body of manifestation.

[38] The veil which surrounded the Plêrôma or World of Divine
Ideas was called "Stauros" (Cross) and Horos (Boundary). *Cp.*
Hippolytus (vi. 3): "Now it is called 'Boundary' because it bounds
off the Deficiency from the Fullness [so as to make it] exterior
to it. It is called Partaker because it partakes of the Deficiency as
well; and it is called 'Cross' because it hath been fixed immovably
and unchangeably, so that nothing of the Deficiency should be
able to approach the æons within the Fullness."

See also the " Gnôstic Crucifixion," 9, 10, 11 (Acts of
John): "[The Cross] is the defining (or delimitation) of all
things, both the firm necessity of things fixed from things

Universe was moved at the presence of the Lord of the
whole Earth; the Æon was troubled and in suspense
because it had seen that which it knew not. The King
of Glory was seated, He divided matter into two halves
and into two parts.[39] He fixed the borders of each part
and taught them that they came from One Father and
from One Mother. To those who ran unto Him and
adored Him He gave the place at the right hand, and
gave them Life for ever and ever and Immortality. He
named the place on the right "The Land of Life," and
the place on the left "The Land of Death"; He named
the Earth on the right "The Earth of Light," and the
Earth on the left "The Earth of Darkness"; He named
the Earth on the right "The Earth of Repose," and the

unstable, and the harmony of wisdom. And as it is Wisdom in
Harmony, there are those on the Right and those on the Left—
powers, authorities, principalities and dæmons, energies,
threats, powers of wrath, slanderings—and the Lower Root
from which hath come forth the things in genesis. This,
then, is the Cross which by the Word hath been the means of
'Cross-beaming' all things—at the same time separating off
the things that proceed from genesis and those below from
those above, and also compacting them all into one."

The "Mantle" in which the Man is clad and which severs and
orders all things is evidently another aspect of the same idea.

The use of the term "veil" is suggestive, as the term is so often
employed in Hellenistic Mysticism in connection with "Initiation."
Finally, it is just worth noting that it is possible that what Origen
has to say about the self-limitation of God is influenced by the
tradition concerning the Horos or "Boundary."

[39]   This is undoubtedly a reference to the Mystical Crucifixion
so often mentioned in previous notes. It is the Master Symbol
of the Unitive State, of the reconciliation and union of God and

Earth on the left "The Earth of Sorrow." He placed boundaries between them and veils, so that they might not see each other; He gave many Glories to those who had adored Him and gave them dominion over those who had resisted and opposed Him. He extended the World of the Right into many places and placed them [who followed Him] in each hierarchy, in each æon, in each world, in each heaven, in each firmament, in many heavens, in each region, in each space, in each receptacle. He gave them [who had followed Him] laws and delivered unto them commandments, saying, "Keep My sayings and I will give unto you eternal life; I will send Powers unto you, yea, I will strengthen you with mighty spirits, and will give unto you the dominion of your desire: no one shall hinder your will, and you shall bring forth æons, worlds, and heavens. When the intellectual spirits come to dwell in you then shall ye become gods, then shall ye know that ye came forth from God, and then shall ye behold Him within yourselves, in your eternities shall He dwell."

Man, and of the participation of the individual in the Universal. Its presence at this point of the text is most suggestive. The candidate, "the Birth of Matter," stands, mystically at any rate, before the Veil at the Foot of the Cross. To pass the Veil and to enter into the Fullness means being united with the Master in His Passion and Crucifixion.

The Cross is evidently a Tau, and I suggest that the frontispiece may represent this Mystery, the Crucifixion of the Æon, O, upon Staurus, the Cross and the Master being One, AΩ and AΩ. The meaning of XMΓ is unknown. It has been suggested that it is (with EIC ΘEOΣ) a symbol of the Trinity in Unity, or a veil of the Divine Name.

These words spake the Lord of the Universe unto them; then He withdrew Himself from them and hid Himself from them. And those who had been the births of matter rejoiced that their thought had been accomplished; they rejoiced because they had come forth from the narrow and the sad. They prayed unto the Hidden Mystery, saying, "Give us power to create æons and worlds according to the word which Thou hast sworn unto Thy servants, for Thou alone art He who changest not, Thou alone art the Infinite and Boundless One, Thou only art unengendered, born of Thyself, Self-Father, Thou only art Unmoved and Unknowable, Thou only Silence art and Love and Fount of the Universe, Thou only art immaterial and hast no stain, ineffable in Thy generation and inconceivable in Thy manifestation. Hear us, then, O Father Incorruptible, Father Immortal, God of Hidden Beings, sole Light and Life, Alone beyond Vision, only Unspeakable, only Unstainable, only [Foundation] stone of Adamant,[40] sole Primal Being,

[40]   The terms I have translated as "Sole Unstainable," "Sole [Foundation]-stone of Adamant" are "Amiantos," "Adamantos." Besides meaning "unstainable," Amiantos was the name of a pale green stone. Readers interested in the legend of the Graal will recall that the Graal is represented as a green stone in the "Parzival" of Von Eschenbach. "Adamantos" is "diamond." Here and in the account of the Monad as the Metropolis of Monogenes, "filled with men of every race and with all the statues of the king," there is a curious parallel to be found to a happening in the life of Saint Theresa. "Being once in prayer," she says, "the Diamond was represented to me like a flash; although I saw nothing formed, still, it was a

for before Thee nothing was. Hearken unto this prayer which we make unto Him who is concealed in every place. Hear us, send unto us incorporeal spirits that they may dwell with us and teach us that which Thou hast promised unto us; that they may dwell in us and that we may become bodies for them, for it is Thy will that it should thus be. So may it be. Give law unto our work and strengthen it according to Thy will and according to the order of the hidden æons; dispose us according to Thy will, for we are Thine."[41]

And He heard them and sent unto them discerning Powers which knew the order of those who are hidden. He established the Hierarchy like the Hierarchies above and according to the concealed

representation with all clearness how all things are seen in God, and how all are contained in Him. . . . Let us say that the Divinity is like a very lustrous Diamond, larger than all the world, or like a mirror—and all that we do is seen in this Diamond, it being so fashioned that it includes everything within itself, because there is nothing but what is contained in this magnitude."

I have ventured to insert [Foundation] because I think that there is a punning allusion to "Adamas." Cp. Naasene Document: "The 'rock' means Adamas. This is the corner-stone . . . which I insert in the foundation of Zion. By this he means allegorically the plasm of man. For Adamas, who is inserted in the inner Man, and the foundations of Zion are . . . the wall and palisade (sc. Horos) in which is the inner Man."

[41] The prayer seems to be for the transmutation of the members of the order by mystical marriages with their archetypal "selves," that the mysteries of the Crucifixion, Resurrection, Ascension, and of the Descent of the Paraclete may be realised after a certain manner.

order. They began from the base to the summit, so that the building might unite them to their companions. He created the aerial earth as a place of habitation for those who had come forth, so that they might dwell therein until the strengthening of those who are below them; then created He the true habitation in the interior of that, the place of repentance in the interior of that, the antitype of Aerodios; then the place of repentance in the interior of that, the antitype of Autogênes: in this place they baptise themselves in the name of Autogênes, who is God over them, and there are Powers placed in this place over the Fount of the Waters of Life which they make go forth. These are the names of the Powers who are over the Waters of Life: Michar and Micheu; and they baptise in the name of Barpharanges. In the interior of these Spaces are the æons of Sophia; in the interior of these Spaces is the True Truth, and Pistis Sophia is found there and also the pre-existent Jesus the Living, Aerodios and his twelve æons. There are placed in this space Sellaô, Eleinos, Zogenethêles, Selmelche, and the Autogênes of the æons. There are placed in him four lights: Èlêlthêth, Daueithe, Ôroiaêl. . . .[42]

[42] Compare this passage with what has already been said concerning an attempt to form an Ideal Order. "A place of Metanoia" implies here a radical change of the whole being rather than "repentance" as ordinarily understood. The "topos" of Autogênes, the Self-begotten, was the first station of the journey of the Light-Spark without the Plêrôma, and is the last station of the return within.

The extant *Gospel of Mary* (Codex Akhmim), which was

He saith:[43]

O Alone-begotten of Light, I praise Thee.

O Light unengendered, I praise Thee.

O Light self-begotten, I praise Thee.

"reviewed" by Irenæus, and was therefore composed before 180 A.D., states that from the Light of the Christ and the Incorruptible proceed forth four great Lights to surround Autogênes. Their names are Harmozel, Oroiael, Daveithi, and Eleleth. Irenæus says, "Charis [Grace] was conjoined with the great and first Luminary, and this they will have to be the Saviour and call him Harmogen"—the Harmes-begotten. The name "Harmes" appears in the present MS., and is evidently a name for Barbêlô. These things are important for the date of the Greek original. The allusions to Pistis-Sophia are probably interpolated; there seems to be no room for her adventures in the scheme of the text. But what are we to make of the mysterious "Baptism in the name of Barpharanges"? Does "Barpharanges" (the meaning of which no one seems to know) simply = Harmogenes = the begotten from Barbêlô), "the Virginal Spirit," the Image seen in the "pure water of Light"? If so, then we have in all probability an allusion to the Gnôstic Baptism with the Holy Spirit or Light. "Harmogenes" will be the Child of the Mystical Marriage with the Virginal Spirit by which the "Spiritual" recover their true manhood, a "blessed æon of æons": that is to say, that the Epopt himself is mystically "Autogênes," the "Self-begotten," having been reborn a god in God.

The rest of the text is missing.

[43]   This Hymn to the Light seems to stand in some close connection with the text we have been discussing. If what has been suggested concerning the contents of the Greek

O Forefather of Light, more excellent than every Forefather, I praise Thee.

O Light Invisible, who art before all those beyond vision, I praise Thee.

O Thought of Light surpassing all Thought, I praise Thee.

O God of Light above all gods, I praise thee.

O Gnôsis of Light passing all knowledge, I praise Thee.

O Unknowable One of Light, who art beyond all that is unknown, I praise Thee.

O Hermit of the Light, who art above all solitaries, I praise Thee.

O All-mighty of the Light, more excellent than the all-powered ones, I praise Thee.

original should prove correct, both the nature and position of the Hymn become plain. It consists of various acts of the will not altogether unlike some of those prescribed in certain Catholic manuals for those in the Unitive way. It is the form of Prayer given by the "Director" or "Master" to his disciple, to be used together with the MS. as part of his preparation for, what I believe to be, the "Baptism of Light." A large part of the Hymn seems to be missing owing to the state of the MS., and the order is uncertain.

O Thou Thrice-mighty of the Light, greater than them of Triple-might, I praise Thee.

O Light that none can separate, for Thou dividest all light, I praise Thee.

O Thou Pure Light, surpassing all purity, I praise Thee.

O Thou who hast begotten [Thyself] in the absence of all generation, Whom none has engendered, I praise Thee.

O Fount of the Universality of Æons, I praise Thee.

O True Self-born of Light, who art before all those self-born, I praise Thee.

O Thou True Unmoved One of Light, who by Thy Will movest all things, I praise Thee.

O Silence of all things, Silence of Light, I praise Thee.

O Saviour of all things, Saviour of Light, I praise Thee.

O Thou Unconquerable One of Light, I praise Thee.

O Thou Sole Space of all the places of the Universe, I praise Thee.

O Thou Only Universal Mystery, I praise thee. O Thou Only All-perfect Light, I praise Thee.

O Thou Only Wise One and Sole Wisdom, I praise Thee.

O Thou Only Intangible, I praise Thee.

O Thou True Goodness, who hast made appear all good things, I praise Thee.

O Thou True Light, who hast made all lights to shine, I praise Thee.

O Thou who sustainest all light and givest life to every soul, I praise Thee.

O Thou Repose of them [? Who seek repose], I praise Thee.

O Thou [Father] of all Paternity from the beginning unto this day, I praise Thee.

They [? Thy children] search for Thee because Thou art their [Father]. Hear the prayer of [Thy children], for [Thou art He who is hidden] in every place, He who is the [Desire] of all hearts.

SUGGESTED READING

Texts

Baynes, Charlotte A. *A Coptic Gnostic Treatise Contained in the Codex Brucianus [Bruce Ms. 96. Bod. Lib, Oxford] A Translation from the Coptic: Transcript and Commentary.* London: Cambridge University Press, 1933.

Robinson, James M., ed. *The Nag Hammadi Library in English.* Translated and Introduced by Members of the Coptic Gnostic Library Project of the Institute for Antiquity and Christianity, Claremont, California. Third, completely revised edition with an Afterword by Richard Smith. San Francisco: HarperCollins, 1988. Important for both the translations and Smith's paper, "The Modern Relevance of Gnosticism."

Schmidt, Carl, ed. *The Books of Jeu and the Untitled Text in the Bruce Codex.* Translation and Notes by Violet MacDermot. Leiden: Brill Academic, 1978 [Nag Hammadi Studies, Volume XIII].

Studies

Layton, Bentley, ed. *The Rediscovery of Gnosticism.*
   Proceedings of the International Conference on
   Gnosticism at Yale . . . 1978. 2 vols. [Studies in
   the History of Religions, XLI] Volume 1, "The
   School of Valentinus"; Volume 2, "Sethian
   Gnosticism." Leiden: Brill Academic, 1980.
Pétrement, Simone. *A Separate God: The*
   Christian Origins of Gnosticism. San Francisco:
   HarperSanFrancisco, 1984. A powerful
   counterbalance to much recent, and woolly,
   writing on the subject.
Williams, Michael Allen. *Rethinking "Gnosticism":*
   An Argument for Dismantling a Dubious
   Category. Princeton: Princeton University
   Press, 1996. An innovative and increasingly
   influential work that forces scholars to
   rethink entrenched attitudes to Gnosis and
   the Gnostics.